I0791328

HIS MARVELOUS LIGHT

THE SECRETS OF THE KINGDOM

W.D. BROUGHTON

Archway Publishing books may be ordered through booksellers or by contacting:

Archway Publishing
1663 Liberty Drive
Bloomington, IN 47403
www.archwaypublishing.com
844-669-3957

ISBN: 978-1-6657-0933-0 (sc)
ISBN: 978-1-6657-0932-3 (hc)
ISBN: 978-1-6657-0934-7 (e)

Library of Congress Control Number: 2021913696

Print information available on the last page.

Archway Publishing rev. date: 10/14/2021

"Then was the secret revealed unto Daniel in a night vision. Then Daniel blessed the God of heaven.

Daniel answered and said, Blessed be the name of God for ever and ever: for wisdom and might are his:

And he changeth the times and the seasons: he removeth kings, and setteth up kings: he giveth wisdom unto the wise, and knowledge to them that know understanding:

He revealeth the deep and secret things: he knoweth what is in the darkness, and the light dwelleth with him."

Daniel 2:19-23 KJV

CONTENTS

FOREWORD

One of the most exciting times in my life is when I met Willard D. Broughton, III. Living in a rural small town in Alabama, we never heard of a Broughton. So I knew I needed to know who this man was. He was a quiet and mean-looking young man. Never judge a book by its cover! Later, I met David while in Single's Ministry at church. David was the name given to him by his mother. He didn't say much but when he spoke, it was with great knowledge and understanding of the Word of God. I saw a man after God's own heart and a true servant of God. Is he perfect? No, but neither am I. We all are imperfect servants of God. From the very start, I knew something was different about him. From the outside, you see an ordinary man but he is more than what you see on the outside. In 2017, we were licensed by our pastor, Byron P. Franklin, Sr. of Living Word Church-Livingston, AL. He would tell you that God licensed him at a very young age. He believes that God's approval is much more important than man's approval. I watch in awe of what the Lord is doing in his life. I didn't realize until later that he would be the one that hears the audible voice of God. This was confirmed to him by a church member Sonjilyn Benn. With deep divine revelation knowledge downloaded from God, he brings the Bible to present-day victories. We are more than who men say we are; we are much more. These are the words that he echoes daily. For years, I knew something was missing in our teachings and I can see the Bible unveiled through his teaching. He has knowledge that can only be revealed by God. To understand that God's plan for mankind is so more than what our parents, teachers, friends, or even our pastors told us for many years. In this book, he walks believers and non-believers through the Bible to share what was revealed to him in a Day to Day conversation with God.

Minister Joyce Jackson-Broughton, wife
Co-Owner of LIT Ministry

PREFACE

There are very few revelatory teachings that deal with the many different races of humankind and their many skin pigmentations. The Bible speaks on the separation of man's language from one common language into many different languages but doesn't deal with the different hues of the human skin. At least not in the books of the Bible that are commonly known as the 66 books classified as the Old and New Testaments.

There are other books in the Lost Scrolls of the Bible that deal with the different nationalities more closely. However, none deal with why we are shaded so differently that we all incorrectly define our brother and falsely prejudge one another. As a result, we even kill one another all because our selfish, sinful nature doesn't want people of another nationality to get ahead or advance above the nationality that we were born into. We are all this way by what we call "instinct" but in this book, "His Marvelous Light," the Holy Spirit will show us how this instinctive nature really is the sinful nature that we inherited from Satan himself.

The Holy Spirit took me by the hand through the Holy Bible from Genesis to Revelation and revealed to me not only why we are shaded

many different colors and divided into many different groups or nationalities, but He also revealed the Secrets of the Kingdom. This is a part
of his perfect plan of reconciliation from the flood of Noah's ark to the
Holy Rapture. Shortly after this detailed walk through the Bible, the
Holy Spirit instructed me to write this vision of Light down and make it
plain so that others can see it and run with it. The Holy Spirit then told
me that He loves and has a purpose for all men, Jews, and Gentiles until
all the nations of the Earth are blessed.

ACKNOWLEDGEMENT

would like to thank my wife Joyce Broughton for her encouraging words to me after she read through the first rough draft of this book. After three years I still remember how she turned her head away from the pile of papers on her lap to look me in the eye to say "David this doesn't make any sense." However, I was thankful to learn that the misunderstanding was due to grammatical errors and not the context.

Over the years this book's pathway to completion grew cold partially because of a hectic work schedule and probably due to my wife's encouraging words. At any rate, there were other people like my mother Emma Palmer and my church daughter Alexandria Cunningham who constantly reminded me about this book I was supposed to complete. This drove me to have my manuscript professionally edited by Shelly Mascia of Shelley's Editing Service who beautifully transformed my writing into masterful literature.

Last but not least I would like to thank my brother Joseph Palmer for giving his insightful input. My sons Princeton Jackson and Jawayne Murdock along with my brother-in-law's Robert James Jr. and Timothy

James. These young men asked me some of the very hard questions that I inturn asked God for the answer on their behalf. This book HIS MARVELOUS LIGHT The Secrets of the Kingdom is God's answer to their questions.

PROLOGUE

The lust for power manifested itself in eternity amidst perfection sparking a viral outbreak of self-centeredness. This contagious virus was quickly spread by many seductive lips that twisted angelic minds causing them to see Light differently. Their thirst for power caused them to war against The Light to possess it. However, they were defeated by The Light to be banished from perfection onto earth that mankind would be created to have dominion over. Still thirsty for power the leader of these now demonic hosts uses his seductive lips to infect mankind with this deadly lust for preeminence. Through many perilous parallels down through the history of mankind, the effect of this contagious heavenly conflict constantly plays itself over again. However, hidden away from hell and mankind are sealed secrets that have been reserved by The Light to defeat the darkness. Racism, social injustice, and oppression are not ready for what is about to be unearthed and revealed by His Marvelous Light.

WHAT IS LIGHT

Light is the Revealed knowledge of the Word of God who is Christ Jesus, our Lord. This knowledge is not based on mental reasoning, but it's the same Knowledge that was given to Simon Bar Jonas by The Holy Spirit after Jesus asked His Disciples, "Who do men say that I AM?" After they had given their answers, He asked them, "Now who do you say that I AM." Jesus asked them in so many words "What knowledge do you have of me beyond what you can hear me say, or most importantly, see me do?"

Matthew 16:13-20 New International Versions (NIV)
Peter Declares That Jesus Is the Messiah
13 When Jesus came to the region of Caesarea Philippi, he asked his disciples, "Who do people say the Son of Man is?"
14 They replied, "Some say John the Baptist; others say Elijah; and still others, Jeremiah or one of the prophets."
15 "But what about you?" he asked. "Who do you say I am?"

16 Simon Peter answered, "You are the Messiah, the Son of the living God."
17 Jesus replied, "Blessed are you, Simon son of Jonah, for this was not revealed to you by flesh and blood, but by my Father in heaven. 18 And I tell you that you are Peter,[a] and on this rock, I will build my church, and the gates of Hades [b] will not overcome it. 19 I will give you the keys of the kingdom of heaven; whatever you bind on earth will be [c] bound in heaven, and whatever you loose on earth will be[d] loosed in heaven." 20 Then he ordered his disciples not to tell anyone that he was the Messiah.

Simon had the light of revelation knowledge revealed to him by the Spirit of God about Jesus His son. Jesus quickly blessed Simon. Jesus renamed him, Peter after he had made it clear to Peter and the rest of His Disciples that Peter couldn't have thought this on his own. There are things about the spiritual qualities of God's Word that are impossible for the carnal mind to even think of for a man to even give an educated guess on the issues about the spirit world. The Light of God is the actual Rock that Jesus said His Church would be built on, not just on the concrete written scripture alone.

2 Cor.3:3NLT
³ Clearly, you are a letter from Christ showing the result of our ministry among you. This "letter" is written not with pen and ink, but with the Spirit of the living God. It is carved not on tablets of stone, but on human hearts.

This doesn't mean Jesus came to do away with the written word, but rather for His Church, to have a better understanding of the written word by the Holy Spirit. The Holy Spirit imparts spiritual enlightenment on what we can see in HIS written Word so that we can begin to visualize that which the human eye can't see in the spiritual realm.

Isaiah 55:8-9 KJV
8 For my thoughts are not your thoughts, neither are your ways my ways, saith the Lord.
9 For as the heavens are higher than the earth, so are my ways higher than your ways, and my thoughts than your thoughts.

KNOWLEDGE of what we can't see, based on a scripture that we can see, can only be revealed to us by the HOLY SPIRIT. Everything that God wants us to know about Him and His Kingdom can't be written in totality. It is impossible for a mortal man limited to the confines of time to write a book about all the spiritual aspects of eternity. God gave us the Written Word, (the Torah), to give us a recorded account of things that happened all the way up to when Jesus ascended into Heaven.

The Bible ends with The Revelation of Jesus meaning that just because the Written Word in the form of Jesus's human body had ascended, didn't mean that Jesus was done teaching. God was telling us is that now is the time for the Holy Spirit to shine a light on the opaque, human body of Jesus who represents the seen written Word of God. Jesus who was not even translucent before in the flesh now becomes as transparent as a deep ocean of clear water in the spirit. The apostles saw Jesus in this manner on the Mount of Transfiguration, but they didn't understand what the bright light of the Holy Spirit was revealing, so they were afraid. They didn't understand that Jesus, or the Word, is more than just the surface-level skin, flesh, and bone of this natural world. Instead, it is an eternal sea of wisdom, knowledge, and understanding of the Spiritual World.

This wisdom, knowledge, and understanding of Jesus is the LIGHT that shines throughout Jesus's transparent spiritual body to expose the many different layers of God's knowledge. This Light beams through the never-ending depths of Jesus' omniscience and leads us into all truths. Who better to tell of all these mysterious secrets of God than the very transparent Spirit of God Himself, the Holy Spirit.

Jesus told His disciples, "I go and become unseen so you can know my eternal unseen qualities. Then My Holy Spirit will come and help you understand the part of my Word that is invisible to the human eyes.

First, Jesus came to give us evidence of him as a physical man, to reveal the physical, written word. Second, after the physical, written word had been revealed, His human body was then crucified on a Roman cross. Third, after his flesh had died, it was placed in a cave much like the Dead Sea Scrolls. Last like the Dead Sea scrolls He was uncovered and resurrected by the Holy Spirit. Then, after residing on earth with man for forty days and nights, the seen tangible Word, ascended to Heaven where He cannot be seen. Jesus then sent his Holy Spirit, who is Jesus in His unseen form, to reveal to us the unseen realm that we can't understand by just simply reading the written Word of God. The unseen realm of the spirit is really the realm that God wants us to know about. He wants to reveal those unseen qualities about him that have been a kept secret from us so that we may know him as a Spiritual God, instead of *Just* a physical man that walked the earth. We have the opportunity to know Jesus far more than the Apostles did because they only saw him in his fleshly form. However, it is better for us who have not seen just as the Scripture has said. There is unlimited knowledge about the qualities of Jesus's Spirit that can be revealed to the renewed mind of the believer by the Light of The Holy Spirit. As Jesus continues to give us Devine knowledge of the Word through His Holy Spirit, we come to know Him and ourselves better by realizing that we really are made in HIS IMAGE AND LIKENESS. Everything, including our universe, was based on the basic structure of God which is working from the inside out. God desires to get to know us better by us casting all our cares and concerns upon Him, so He can search out the true intentions of our hearts. In other words: if we delight ourselves in the Lord, He will give us the desires of our hearts.

John 15:7 New International Version (NIV)
7 If you remain in me and my words remain in you, ask whatever you wish, and it will be done for you.

John 16:7-15 (NIV)
7 But very truly I tell you, it is for your good that I am going away. Unless I go away, the Advocate will not come to you; but if I go, I will send him to you. 8 When he comes, he will prove the world to be in the wrong about sin and righteousness and judgment: 9 about sin, because people do not believe in me; 10 about righteousness, because I am going to the Father, where you can see me no longer; 11 and about judgment, because the prince of this world now stands condemned.
12 "I have much more to say to you, more than you can now bear. 13 But when he, the Spirit of truth, comes, he will guide you into all the truth. He will not speak on his own; he will speak only what he hears, and he will tell you what is yet to come. 14 He will glorify me because it is from me that he will receive what he will make known to you. 15 All that belongs to the Father is mine. That is why I said the Spirit will receive from me what he will make known to you."

Jesus knew that he wouldn't have time to tell all that he did and even if he did he wouldn't have time to explain it to us as he explained it to His Disciples. So, he sent us His Holy Spirit to teach it to us plainly and not in riddles like when he taught man on Earth. The Light of Truth is heard, rather than seen. This is how God reveals himself to men living in ignorance. The knowledge of God's truth shines a light on our ignorance. This gives us wisdom, knowledge, and understanding of His word. This provides the nourishment that our soul needs to live abundantly and fruitfully.

As a result, our soul begins to prosper. Then our bodies manifest that spiritual prosperity in this physical earthly realm through our tangible works and accomplishments. This is how we are transformed from the inside out to the point that we are no longer even considered to be the same person in the sight of God. We have been totally transformed into new creatures.

Jesus, who is the second Adam, will name us according to our spiritual gifts just like the first Adam did for His wife and all the different creatures of the world. Jesus renamed Simon to Peter, meaning the stone or rock, and was evidence of Peter's ability to hear the Holy Spirit of God. The Holy Spirit has given us all who believe that Jesus Christ is Lord; as a gift or a stone from His very being as an inheritance. The significance of this stone is revealed to us by the Holy Spirit and its qualities reflect exactly who we are as a son or daughter of God. His perfect will and plan for our lives revolve around this stone. This is what the Apostle Paul speaks of as your Spiritual Gift.

In the following chapters, you will learn how your stone, which is your gift of light, fits into the organized body that the New Jerusalem is built upon. In the ancient Jewish culture, stones were handed down to their children as an inheritance. These stones were a reminder of what God did for them and who they were in God.

The Revelation 2:17 TLB
[17] "Let everyone who can hear, listen to what the Spirit is saying to the churches: Everyone who is victorious shall eat of the hidden manna, the secret nourishment from heaven; and I will give to each a white stone, and on the stone will be engraved a new name that no one else knows except the one receiving it."

This scripture alone is proof that in the last days the Holy Spirit will begin to reveal those hidden things about the Word of God to all the seven Churches. A stone will be given to each of the seven churches by their Spiritual Gift. This Spiritual Gift is what Rev. 2:17 TLB is referring to as the new name that nobody else knows except the one who is receiving it. You must discern your spiritual gifts to know what name God has named your Spiritual man so you may know your spiritual name just like you know your common name. To know the name of your Spirit man means that you know the will and purpose God has for your spiritual man. This might be the gift of healing or any of the many manifested gifts of the Holy Spirit.

Therefore, we must develop our spiritual ears so that we can hear whenever the Holy Spirit calls us to work the wonders of these supernatural gifts before men to bring him glory. So let EVERYONE who can hear the Holy Spirit LISTEN. That word LISTEN refers to what He told us in Mark 4:24 of the NIV. Then he added, "PAY CLOSE ATTENTION TO WHAT YOU HEAR." Because the closer you listen, the more revelation you will be given, and you will receive even more revelation knowledge beyond that. Rev. 2:17 *TLB* also states that "EVERYONE who is VICTORIOUS shall eat of the hidden manna". That word victorious is speaking of the seed that fell on good soil representing those who hear the word and accept it gladly. These are the people who will be able to produce much fruit from that one little seed of revealed knowledge as much as thirty, sixty, and even a hundredfold from that one revealed word. All of this is referring back to Mark 4:20 of the NIV. Then as we read further into Rev. 2:17 *TLB* we learn that the revealed knowledge of the Holy Spirit is the hidden manna; the secret nourishment from Heaven that fell and covered the ground in its physical form like frost was given to feed the Children of Israel. Manna in its physical form represents the Written Word or the bread of life. Later on, we learn as Jesus quotes from the book of Deuteronomy in ***Matthew 4:4 KJV that man shall not live by bread alone or the written word but by every word that proceeds out of the mouth of God.*** This represents the revealed word that was given to Simon. The Revealed Knowledge of God was the stone that was given to Simon and on this stone was inscribed Simon's new name, Peter. This spiritual nourishment given to the Church is the same secret manna that sustained Jesus through his 40 day fast in the wilderness when Satan tried to tempt him by asking Jesus to turn these stones into bread.

In Rev. 2:17 TLB, Jesus imparted a little insult to injury to Satan by giving us this secret revelation in the form of a white stone. These stones are given to us so that Satan cannot prevail against us, consume or eat us. Satan always tries to tempt us to do things that seemingly benefit us, but his ultimate desire is always to sustain himself from our Godly nutrients. This is why Jesus tells us that Satan desires to sift us as wheat. This is what Satan desired to do to Jesus' fleshly body in the wilderness, so he could obtain power by gaining access to God's secret revelation knowledge.

This revelation knowledge can only be given to those that God names as His children because the nutrients within the bread of Spiritual Revelation Knowledge are the same nutrients that were in the fruit from the Tree of Life. Therefore, healing is called the "children's bread" and Jesus wouldn't give the bread of God's children to a Dog like Satan. Jesus knew that just like He hungered physically because of obedience to God, Satan hungered even more spiritually because he disobeyed God. Jesus, in total obedience to his Father, didn't turn the stone into physical bread to sustain His earthly cravings. Instead, He took the Spiritual Bread of the LIGHT giving and life-sustaining revelation knowledge of God and made it stone. Jesus then takes these stones and gives them to us as an inheritance of LIFE. What Jesus was implying to Satan was that if you once again bow down in obedience and worship me you can eat the Secret Manna but until then feast your eyes upon these Stones. These life-giving stones are only for those who are my children. This means that His Children are the only ones who can listen and understand the Revealed Knowledge of the Children's bread. Actually, Jesus is asking Satan, "can you ingest and digest these stones of revelation knowledge, because this is the only way to partake of the bread of life". This is how God prepares a table of Revelation knowledge for us in the presence of our enemy Satan. God knows his children are the only creatures who can ingest and digest these stones. Healing is the Children's bread. God gave Moses special instruction concerning his Manna, so it wouldn't be any leftovers for Satan. We know throughout the Bible that God is very particular when it comes to his life-sustaining bread; this is why any bread kept until the next day would rot. So like Simon whose name was changed to Peter, we who hear the Word of God and do what it says will be given a white stone as an inheritance from the Holy Spirit, who is the Light of truth. With this inheritance of the secret healing nourishment, we let this light shine before men so that they can see our good works, then glorify our Father who is in heaven.

Those Good Works that we display in the natural are miracles, signs, and wonders. We are the light of the world, which is the manifestation of God's Spiritual Revelation knowledge and power magnified through our carnal bodies. Now, we who are being transformed by the Light, have become like the Tree mentioned in Psalms Chapter 1. As we meditate or absorb this light, our leaf will not wither and whatever we do shall prosper. Jesus, who is the LIGHT OF THE WORLD, told us "EVEN GREATER WORKS SHALL WE DO THAN THESE."

THE SYNERGETIC TOWER OF BABEL

I asked the Holy Spirit why we are shaded in different colors. The Holy Spirit revealed to me what could be described as a highly graphic movie complete with all the special effects. In my mind's eye, He took me back to Genesis. I saw a glorious city filled with proud people. In the middle of this city was a triangular-shaped tower that seemed to gleam in the sunlight.

"This is Babel," He said. "That high and lofty tower is a symbol of the people's pride that began to exalt itself against me. This is the same pride that rose amid their father Satan and exalted itself against my throne. The leader of this arrogance was Nimrod, who was a great hunter. His name means enlightenment. He instructed the people to build this tower into the heavens as a testament of themselves to bring fame or the LIGHT OF GLORY to themselves."

Then the Holy Spirit began to tell me, "Pride bends My Glory back upon man and I share my Glory with no one." This is the reason man's common language had to be cast down.

The Holy Spirit said, "I really didn't confound man's language. Man did it to himself. The secret to the confusion and separation of men lies with this tower of pride that was built for their Glory. I AM NOT the author of Confusion."

Then He told me, "The First thing you have to understand is I AM the LIGHT of the World that Shines because of my LIFE. Because I AM LIFE, you are LIGHT also." He explained to me that every man that ever originated on Earth is LIGHT, speaking of your SPIRIT, not your Flesh. Your Spirit is your Light that originated from one source and that source is MY TRUTH. My light is TRUTH. I AM the only TRUE and LIVING GOD. Why does MY TRUTH admit LIGHT? Because my TRUTH is FIRE. My Fire burns bright with the TRUE KNOWLEDGE that gives every living thing POWER. KNOWLEDGE IS POWER and I have KNOWLEDGE of ALL and so I possess ALL POWER.

The Holy Spirit told me that ALL POWER admits light or Glory. My Glory is the LIGHT of the World. I created the earth and MAN for MY GLORY, which is my LIGHT. Earth and Man prosper with my LIGHT. Without it, both will surely die. Therefore, my people suffer for a LACK of Light, which is the KNOWLEDGE of MY TRUTH.

HE said, "David Notice I said they suffer for a LACK of LIGHT, just like a plant that is shaded from the sun. Whatever you came from, you must be continually connected to, to live eternally. Man shaded and separated himself from my LIGHT by his pride. That is represented by this tower that man is building here in Babel. Now, do you see David why man is separated from me?"

As I looked at the shape of this vast object, I no longer saw a brick-and-mortar tower. Instead what I saw was a shiny, transparent prism towering from the earth. *Wow*, I thought *how in the world could prehistoric people have the technology to make a tower made of crystal glass?* The Holy Spirit told me, "David, what you are seeing is what the tower represents in the spiritual realm, THE REALM OF LIGHT. The tower is made of stone, brick, and mortar in the flesh, but it's a shiny crystal glass prism in the Spirit Realm."

The Holy Spirit explained once again that an earthly object itself has no spirit. However, this tower possesses the Spirit of everyone involved in building it. The tower stands in the spiritual realm as a dividing spirit of pride because the people are unified, and their spirit is one. The fleshly man was not who I was concerned about reaching Heaven, but it was the spirit of the people as one that could accomplish anything they set their Hearts to do.

This tower is also an example of what can be manifested in the spirit realm by everyone in The Body of Christ coming together, in My Name on one accord. MY NAME IS A STRONG TOWER that the righteous run into and are saved. My tower is a tower of TRUTH that Gives or Admits MY LIGHT so that every man that comes into it shall live. Satan's tower of pride takes MY TRUTH or MY LIGHT and bends my light back on himself so that He may appear as an angel of light. "What happens when you bend or pervert the Truth?" the Holy Spirit asked. "It becomes a lie," I answered. "Correct," the Holy Spirit stated. "These people and all of mankind have believed the lie of Satan telling man that he doesn't need God. That he can do it all himself, giving man an instinctive false hope that I call "pride". David, you see the results of this instinctive behavior throughout the world. Man has become a slave to his own pride causing him to hate and kill his brother because he must feed his pride. Pride is a harsh and greedy taskmaster that never gets enough. Creation suffers because of man's pride, which shines as the false light from Satan, the fallen angel. Satan absorbs the pride to make himself look Glorious in man's eye; so that he appears to possess all things so that man will accept him and reject the true Possessor of Heaven and Earth.

Man pursues the road to destruction because Satan has given him false hope. In actuality, it is My light that has been twisted by this beast telling man that my possessions are his. Look how many follow their lusts and desires in hopes of something that is nothing more than a lie. The end of the road is destruction and death."

These people are building a representation of the fallen angel himself who still in this day desires to ascend to my throne through men. Satan desired my life by separating me with his prism of pride to take my throne. Instead through humility, I counteracted this plot by giving my life by using man's prism of pride to divide my light. I didn't give My Life unto death as my Son did in the flesh but as a living gift. When I came down from Heaven it was not to confuse man but to give man what he desired from Me and more. I worked my principles of Humility that say give to anyone who begs of you and if anyone takes your coat give him your cloak as well. In this same manner, my servant Elijah gave his servant Elisha his cloak which represented a double portion of the mantle of gifts that I had given to Elijah. I gave men My coat of light including My cloak before he could exercise power over me by taking it. However, what I intended to be a blessing to men became a curse to him because of their pride. This Prism which you see towering toward Heaven like a sword out of the depths of hell separated my light into many shades rationing my life for many. Men could not see me clearly like Elisha saw Elijah as his mantle was given because their pride had divided my light in their eyes. As a result of my gift to men being divided, they became confused. Men had become acclimated to Satan's system of pride and did not understand how the one all-powerful God would be willing to give His life in humility. By being humble I saved my life by giving it which is the essence of my principle that states that whoever saves his life will lose it but whoever loses his life will keep it. Men whose ways were orchestrated by Satan sought to take my Life by separating my Light the same way the Roman soldiers tried to separate my Son's seamless robe at Calvary. Satan knows that I AM THE LIGHT and he wanted to use his prism of pride to divide my light as he did to the third of heaven before he was cast out. If Satan could twist my truth with his pride, he could get my Holy Angels to form different opinions of me. A house divided against itself will not stand. David, once a spirit forms an opinion about the Truth, they pervert that Truth even more by spreading it to other spirits in the form of gossip. This causes those spirits to form their own opinions about me and the lie begins to spiral. This is how Satan corrupted so many of my angels and the spirits of mankind. Once Satan perverted MY truth in the eyes and the ears of my people, they formed their own opinion of Me. By trying to form their own truth they became even more separated from My Truth.

Throughout the Generations, the Truth has all but been forgotten. Through science, man uses the natural earth to try to find cures and answers that can only be revealed to them by a supernatural God. I AM the answer; I AM the Way, The Truth, and The Life, but man continues to search. You, however, David have sought to find the truth at its source. I'm going to reveal to you what they have been trying to find out for generations.

You, just like all these people, are spirits that originated from My Light. It might sound foolish to you, but you are light. From now on, I will refer to your spirit as light. This is who you really are. The earthen vessel that is your flesh enables your light to be recognized on this earth. Without it, your light could not be seen by other human beings. Your spirit is the light and your flesh is the lamp. Your flesh manifests whatever lives within it. This means the lamp does not give light before the wick is lit. Then, after the wick is lit, the flame of fire brings the lamp to life. Now, the lamp, or the flesh allows the light from the fire to shine before men.

Your lamp which is your flesh once gave full reverence to the light that resided inside of it. It radiated this unadulterated one pure light of Truth. Glorious in all its ways, man's carnal body Glowed with my Truth with a fire that did not consume man's flesh as with the burning bush of Moses. Earthly fire consumes, however, my fire of Truth Glorifies and protects. At that moment that you are transfigured, you will once again have a Glorified Body. My truth that lives inside of you will now be transparent throughout your body as the fire within a lamp. My Truth will be revealed once again for creation to see."

The Holy Spirit told me, "Fire is made from my truth. The reason why My fire does not consume is that I am what fire is. As I told Moses, "I AM that I Am" and a house divided against itself will not stand. Does fire burn fire, David? No. My fire only consumes sin. It can't stand to be in my presence because the heat of my fiery truth irritates sin. When Adam sinned, it caused the whole earth to be cursed just like man's flesh. Because of that, they can't stand to feel the heat from my truth or they will both be consumed. If you need evidence, look on top of my Holy Mountain."

Then the Holy Spirit laughed. "Now you tell me why the Children of Israel couldn't come close to My Mountain? Tell me, David. Why does Hell's Fire torment sin? If you made your bed in Hell, I would be there with you. Why? Because my very fire of truth that torments evil would protect you; who have been made righteous through Jesus."

"I AM that FIRE David. I AM the Holy Specter or the Holy Spirit. The FIRE OF THE HOLY SPIRIT is the TRUTH. The LIGHT that Radiates from it is the knowledge of THE Truth. Within this light are many different gifts that are given to each man but all are of the same Truth or they all originated from the same fire. Look again at this tower and tell me what you see David."

"I see a rainbow of colors," I answered.

"Yes with each color representing the different Gifts of the SPECTRUM unseen to the human eye, manifested by each human operating gracefully in that specific area of their gift. Just like the many different colors of the plants, soils, and clouds, they were all made to reflect my awesome light of truth. They all have different colors to show that they serve a different purpose in my will. The fallen angel Lucifer had many gifts and talents represented by the colorful priceless stones that were a part of his very makeup."

The many colors of his priceless stones complemented his gifts better than any fashion designer could imagine. While possessing all of these gifts Lucifer didn't even have a third of the gifts and talents that lie within the truth of my knowledge.

He had the grace to Dance, sing, and worship me in the beauty of Holiness. However, instead of reflecting or magnifying my light of truth to Glorify Me, he used those gifts which were designed for my Glory to glorify himself.

This is what sin is David; using the gifts that I gave you to glorify me for yourself. My fire consumes sin. My truth is a double-edged sword: if you love it and live by it, then it can go before you, bless you, and make room for you.

On the other edge, you will feel the sharpness of the truth. If you refuse to hear the word and heed it, the very truth that was meant to bless you will curse you. However, always remember that it was never my decision. The choice was yours to decide which side of the double-edged sword of truth you stand on. My truth is constant, it never changes and it is always the same.

There is no evil side to my sword of truth. My truth is just, pure, and righteous through and through. Man chooses. Just like Lucifer chose. Either stand behind my Sword and let it fight for you or to be against My Sword and commit spiritual suicide. Hell is a decision, not a verdict. Once again, the Fire of Truth can either be a part of your glorified body like your clothing. Or it can remind you constantly of what is just and right. . My constant truth will burn for eternity whether for purification and glorification or torment and damnation.

David, man was clothed with my fire of Truth. My truth girded man's loins physically. It was a manifestation that man was clothed in his right mind Spiritually because everything that is within the mind of man manifested through his flesh. Your flesh is a manifestation of your spirit. It enhances who you are on the outside by displaying to the world your gifts and talents in the same full color that I have given your spirit on the inside. This is why you prosper as your soul prospers.

The lamp, which is your body, enhances the light and gives the light a physical body and hue. This enables that light to be noticed and light up your surroundings. This light is the tool for your unique gifts represented by hues or different shades of colors. Now great people will notice you because of the GOOD works it enables you to do. Then, after they see your GOOD WORKS, they will want to do GOOD WORKS themselves. These works will open the soils of their minds so that the GOOD NEWS of the Gospel can be planted within. This seed that is planted in their midst is my light of Truth. So when the seed matures, it will become like the tree that produced the seed.

Then, they too can GLORIFY ME by doing the same for others. This is how my Gospel of Truth will reunite the divisions of my people caused by Gossip or the lie of Satan. Remember how Satan corrupted a third of my Holy Angels with Gossip, which is the LIE. *I, THE LORD GOD, will reconcile the WORLD with the GOSPEL or the Truth. GOSSIP DIVIDES BUT THE GOSPEL UNITES.*

Hue or color is given to every man, representing the uniqueness of his family's gift of light. Through Me, all things were created and nothing was created without Me. Everything that has ever been created can find its origin in my fire of Truth. From the Light of Truth that radiates from my fire are many gifts, talents, and abilities. Each one of them has its own shade of color in the SPECTRUM of the SPIRIT REALM. These colors compliment each other and assist each other just like the organs in your body.

The functions of your organs are exactly how these different colors function within Me. Your family group has a specific spiritual function on the earth, represented by the color of light that is specific to that spiritual gift. The color of that man's gift burns with that specific color of light. Whatever is done in the Spirit, is manifested in the flesh. This means the color of your skin is specific to the gifts and talents given to your specific family of people. Therefore, certain families can do things with ease and be weak in other things. Where one family is the weakest, another family is strong. This doesn't mean that any color is greater than the next. It just means that all the different shades of light must come together and function as a body. Just like the different colors of the rainbow are overlapped to connect one color to the next, your spiritual gifts are also ordered in this fashion so there won't be any weakness. I the Lord have arranged all spiritual gifts according to how it pleases me and that is the order that you must operate in. I have arranged you in such a way so that where you are the weakest, you are made strong. Not because of your gift but because of your brothers' gift to you.

Now let the weak say I am strong and let the poor say I am rich. I, the Lord, have caused your brothers to give unto your bosom. Different groups and nationalities of gifts have different functions in the body. Just like the different organs function differently in your body. As each one of them gives their gift to the next organ, your body becomes strong and you begin to function properly as a whole.

Cain needed his brother Abel. But because of the selfish, competitive nature of sin, Cain saw his brother's gift as a threat instead of a gift for him. What Cain didn't know was why Abel's gift pleased me. What Abel gave was the livestock that was needed for Sacrifice. That was the atonement for both brothers' sins. Yes, this same atonement would be used repeatedly until my son who is the sacrificial lamb became the ultimate atonement for all mankind. Even though my son had to die so that man may live, my son was murdered by his brothers for bearing the same gift as Abel did: the gift of atonement.

However, I knew that the ultimate price of competition was elimination. I planned it so that when they eliminated my Son, they were also enabling him to utilize his hidden gift. Satan realized that my son was a gift of fruit for all men. What Satan didn't realize is that a seed remained after the fruit was consumed. So when they buried my son, Satan didn't know they were planting a seed. Only a seed can be buried and rise again as a tree on the third day. The miracle of the resurrection was the principle of seed, time, and harvest manifested. Satan always comes to kill steal and destroy the gift of the Word. However, this time Satan's plan to kill and eliminate sealed his own fate.

The Tower of Babel represented the division of Gifts. Until then, every man knew how to communicate their differences of gifts in a specific order to their brother who possessed a contrasting gift so that he could understand them. Men could communicate efficiently with one another because they had the same language. If men could communicate in the same language, they could achieve anything that they IMAGINED. So man's perfect communication allowed them to have a mental picture or an image of how the tower would look when it was completed. Their communication allowed each of their minds to be together as one body just like in The HOLY COMMUNION where you partake of the dismembered body of Jesus and it is remembered within you. As each mind joined in with the next, that mental image began to form a solid strong shiny spiritual structure that begins to manifest in the spirit. The result was a spiritual structure in the form of a four-sided, incomplete tower. Each person has a light that originated in my fire of truth. Each light or Spirit has a specific color representing that spiritual gift. You see David; the tower was not complete because each family or group of people had not given of their gift for it to be completed. Some of the family groups or nationalities had given. Some were waiting their turn but each group assisted the other until their specific talent or gift was needed.

It's like a group of contractors looking at the same blueprint. Each contractor, although they are working on the same building, has different roles to play. Some are heavy equipment operators who dig and some are cement layers that lay the foundation. Some are steelworkers who assemble the walls and so on until the building is complete.

At Babel, each person within each family group knew their specific gifts. They knew that for the tower to be finished, they would have to contribute to the construction of the tower. So each person knew that the tower wouldn't be complete until all the nationalities or groups contributed their specific gift. This in turn left a not yet finished tower in the spiritual realm.

Men begin to see my marvelous light through their own prism of sin and that prism separated my light according to their own viewpoints. Now that they all saw me in a different light or color, they could only communicate with me according to that shade of light that corresponded to their gift. They couldn't see me through their brother's eyes of a different nationality; now they could only see me through their eyes. Since they no longer had a common viewpoint they begin to call out to their brothers' names of different gifts or nationalities. However, to their brothers, they now sounded like they were babbling like babies because their gift of tongues had also been divided.

To their own family, they could understand each other perfectly because they all shared the same tongue that is associated with the gifts they shared. Therefore the language that you speak is a gift. All men have different and unique gifts so, in turn, all men speak with different spiritual tongues.

Then the Holy Spirit asked me, "David, what have you learned from my Holy Word? On the day of Pentecost, they were given the ability to understand other tongues. How was that possible? As the Holy Spirit asked me the question, He also revealed to me the answer.

My answer was, "They were in unity, meaning that their gifts were joined together like the people of Babel before they separated their gifts with their prism of pride."

"Yes David," the Holy Spirit replied. "Just like the people of Babel, as long as their many different gifts were joined as one, forming one body, they all spoke the same tongue. But after their different gifts were separated, they begin to speak with the tongue of their common family gift. Directly after this separation, they began to group, according to their own common understanding. So because they couldn't see the same point of view, they formed their own opinion of their brothers and me.

This breakdown of communication was caused by Satan. In this same manner, Lucifer broke down the communication of a third of my angels in heaven by twisting my Light of Truth on himself. All the angels that believed the lie of Lucifer now had different opinions of me like these people leaving this tower. The tower was incomplete because every brother hadn't contributed his spiritual gift to its construction and so it lies incomplete in the spiritual realm."

Now you see that the color of your skin was not to keep you separate but to distinguish you and show off your unique gifts. When all the different nationalities come together to work as one body, they complete that body. After all the members come together, the body that they form in the spirit is a perfect reflection of me because that living body is the BODY of Christ. For He who has seen the SON has also seen the Father.

Your gifts reflect my Light of Truth. Each different creation of God, both living and inanimate, has its own color representing the specific purpose it has on earth. For it to serve that purpose, I have given each a gift that graces them to do it with ease.

I gave man an image of myself as a covenant that can't be seen until the light hits in such a way that shows my beautiful colors. I AM ALL THE GIFTS that I have distributed unto each group or each country. The rainbow consists of seven visible colors with seven other invisible colors. The visible colors represent the physical realm or the earthly realm. The invisible colors represent the spiritual realm or the Heavenly realm. In other WORDS, my gifts of LIGHT that you can't see in the spirit are reflected by earth and the flesh of man.

Man is a direct reflection of me because I made him in my image and my likeness. This is why when you see a rainbow you only see an arch instead of a complete spiral of colors that would form a perfect circle like the rings around Saturn. Just because you can't see the other half of the spiral of colors doesn't mean that they aren't there. It's just that one half represents the Unseen or the Spiritual realm and the other half represents the seen or the physical realm. Just like in the planet Saturn which is a perfect model of what the rainbow is with the seen and unseen parts. Everything in the natural world is a perfect reflection of what's existing in the spirit world.

The word IMAGE means to reflect. I created earth and man not only to reflect but to also magnify or multiply the Light of my Glory back upon ME.

"OH, MAGNIFY THE LORD FOR HE IS WORTHY TO BE PRAISED." Man was supposed to be fruitful and multiply my Spirit in the earth. Instead, man, like Lucifer, uses the gifts that I gave him and perverts them to bring glory to himself.

The human form, beauty, dancing, singing, and even sex in marriage were all created to bring praise and glory to me. However: man, like Lucifer, uses all these things to bring Glory to himself. Man uses my gifts of praise for personal gain. Man gets carried away by his own lust for pleasure and riches to the point that they are willing to do anything to get it. Selling their souls seem cheap compared to the worldly treasures that Satan offers them so that he may be able to hold the deeds to their soul. Satan twists my light upon himself in this same way to get my creation to worship him by using my gifts of praise that I gave man outside of the ordered boundaries that I set in place. Satan goes about as an angel and his light shines bright because he uses my model of praise and raises himself to the point that all of man's focus is on him. Thus crowning Satan as a god in the throne room at the center of man's mind so that all men can glorify him instead of Me.

The light which is your spirit will illuminate whatever god you worship, and others will notice it and worship it as well. This principle of praise and worship is the same whether you use it for evil or good. For example, you can let your light so shine on your perverse lusts and evil deeds so others, in turn, can also use their light which is their life or spirit to glorify Satan; or you can let your life so shine on your good works so others can glorify God instead.

Your Bright Idea is a product of your fleshly mind. The prefix Id in the word idea means reptilian mind and its suffix ea is the Akkadian god of wisdom. Anything of the flesh when not governed by the Spirit of Man automatically resorts back to the mind of its father Satan. Satan is Represented by that sinister, crafty, reptile in the Garden of Eden, THE SERPENT. Satan talked to EVE in the Garden through the snake by using his word which his twisted, opinionated truth is called GOSSIP. Remember this Godly principle, faith comes by hearing the WORD of God. This means the mind of whoever you listen to is imparted to your mind. This is how God transforms your mind into HIS mind by hearing HIS WORD.

God calls HIS WORD THE GOSPEL who IS HIS SON JESUS and IS about HIS SON JESUS. SATAN used God's principle of mind transformation with Eve the same way that he used it on the angels of heaven. Eve listened to SATAN'S WORD which is HIS opinion of God, mixed with a hint of the Truth called Gossip. Satan's Gossip began to take root in Eve's mind. As it grew, she began to have that same opinion about GOD and herself. Eve begins to believe her own opinion over the knowledge of God.

Now once Eve starts to believe the opinion of her newly transformed mind over God's knowledge, in that very instant Satan, became her god. The only thing left for Eve to do now was to worship the lord over her mind by eating the forbidden fruit. Eating the fruit made Eve's rebellion official. This was another Godly principle that Satan used against Eve, which is whatever happens on the inside of a man is manifested on the outside. Whatever is already done in the Spirit is manifested in the flesh.

This same principle can be seen in agriculture. Whatever is planted in the soul of the earth represents what you can't see in the spiritual realm because you can't see a seed once it is planted. Then one day you look out and see a physical manifestation of something that has already gone on in the Spirit. This principle is called Transformation. Eve became a Gossiper as well. In Genesis, it says Adam listened to his wife. We see now how influential and deadly your opinions can be because anything that we hold up in front of God takes God's place in our lives and becomes our god. God calls these idols.

The children of Israel thought that Moses was dead, and God had deserted them. So as a result they built a bright and shiny Golden calf. The Children of Israel erected this calf because once again they believed their own reptilian mind over God's knowledge. The calf stood as a physical manifestation of their opinion in front of God in the Spiritual realm. Even though the Children of Israel had a physical manifestation of this opinion, it's not until they started having sexual orgies in the form of worship that it was made official.

It can be easily seen by observing the Israelites that racism is a god or an idol for the racist. Racism is an idea produced in the small mind of man about his brother or sister of a different skin color which we have learned is a result of their family's Spiritual Gift. His opinion of his brother stands in front of God's KNOWLEDGE and replaces God. The result is man or woman that believes in their image or idol over God's truth about another race.

When they partake of the fruit of their God of racism by acting the hate out in a form of worship, they make it official. Once again, they have become the physical manifestation of the god over their lives. God said, "Cast down those images which are ideas and opinions and hold every one of your reptilian thoughts captive to the obedience of Jesus Christ."

God knew that man's self-image would never benefit himself or his brother. This is because man's carnal mind is selfish and evil just like the mind of Satan that governs it.

Your ideas, your identity, your idols are rooted in your minds. You wouldn't have to find out who you are if you just believe God's word of knowledge over what your fleshly mind is telling you. God said that you were made in my image and my likeness. God's name I AM is where we get the prefix IM. The prefix ID as we've been discussing comes from Satan meaning IT or of a reptilian mind.

So, whatever is the AM, or the governor of your mind, is who you really are. In other words, if the Great I AM is the governor of your mind, you will manifest in the flesh his likeness because you become transformed into HIS IMAGE and LIKENESS simply because your mind is renewed and governed by GOD.

So we don't get it twisted, we won't be physically transformed into God's image and likenesses like Adams and Eve were until we are transfigured. For now, we will display Godlike qualities.

The Word of God teaches it's possible to have other little images before God. This same principle applies to those little images as well. We know what our Image or idol is by the way we act or how we worship it. For example, if the image is racism, we will act out racially or, if it's food or drugs, we will see the results physically.

Why is it this way? Whatever your mind is governed by, you become it to the point that you can look in the mirror and say this is who I AM. This is why you have to be TRANSFORMED BY THE RENEWING OF YOUR MIND IN THE WORD.

Anything that Blocks what God said that is true about any situation, person, place, or thing and leaves you in its dark shadow of ignorance while making you a victim to your own reptilian mind is an idol. It's that high and lofty thing that Blocks God's LIGHT of TRUTH. We perish because of senseless acts of hate. It all stems from us having a LACK OF GOD'S TRUE KNOWLEDGE.

If I am lifted, I will draw all men unto me. To put it plainly, just like the sun's gravity pulls the planets to itself, I will draw men unto me. Who or whatever is in the center of your life is King and everything that happens in the solar system of your life is a direct result of who sits on the throne of your mind. Whether it is a Tree of LIFE or the Tree of the Knowledge of Good and Evil, those that are governed by their specific tree shall eat the fruits of it. Satan exalted himself in heaven. After that, he lifted the serpent in the Garden which caused man to lift his opinion against me. The mind of the serpent now resides in and rules over the mind of man allowing his word of Gossip to be constantly fed unknowingly to the next man. Man has taken on the prideful, lofty nature of the one who possessed the serpent's body: Satan is the orchestrator behind this synergetic tower. The only way to stop Satan's lie is to expose him with the Light of the Word of Truth.

I sent My Light of Truth to men as Emanuel who is the seed of the Woman that will crush the head of the serpent. Jesus, who is the seed of the woman, will crush the entire army of serpent heads gathered around this synergetic tower. When I saw that all the men working on the tower had heads of serpents, I looked away. As I looked away I saw men of this present time and the people all had heads of serpents. My TRUTH will crush the heads of all these serpents which represent every opinion of man with the light of the knowledge of the GOSPEL. The light or the knowledge of the truth crushed the opinions of these men building this synergetic tower and confounded the minds of the fang-toothed vipers, just like your Praise and Worship of Me CONFOUNDS our enemy Satan.

My Truth is confusing to the fleshly animal mind of man. This is why I use parables, so people will hear and see but not understand. "This fulfills the prophecy of Isaiah:

'They hear, but don't understand; they look, but don't see!
Matthew 13:14 NIV

This same principle is what happened to man's communication:

21 For God in his wisdom saw to it that the world would never find God through human brilliance, and then he stepped in and saved all those who believed his message, which the world calls foolish and silly. 1 Corinthians 1:21 TLB

The Holy Spirit spoke to me again. Man's language was tied to his human or reptilian mind from his demise in the Garden up till the building of this tower. Satan took control of this unified tongue and used it to spread his word of Gossip to cause mutiny against me, just like he tried in Heaven This common tongue was Hubris, stemming from man's human brilliance or light. When I came down with my TRUTH in humility man's hubris or his pride was automatically cast down by my wisdom as I said in *1 Corinthians 1:20. TLB*

So, what about these wise men, these scholars, these brilliant debaters of this world's great affairs? God has made them all look foolish and shown their wisdom to be useless nonsense.

You see David, these men can't attempt to reach me through their own brilliance that once unified them. My light has shown man's wisdom to be useless nonsense and their unified pride is what I cast down just like I cast down Satan and all of his followers out of Heaven. Pride, called hubris, was the common language that connected man's communication so that after man could no longer communicate through pride he could no longer try to save himself through his own brilliance. His brilliant Ideas I simply ignored just like all other Gossip and they ceased to exist. Men should handle Gossip by addressing it as GOSSIP, then ignoring it as I did for these people when I freed their minds from Satan's grip so that they could inhabit the whole earth.

1Corinthians 1:19 TLB For God says, "I will destroy all human plans of salvation no matter how wise they seem to be, and ignore the best ideas of men, even the most brilliant of them."

Now that the common language of pride has been terminated the language of every man, is now tied to the spiritual gift of his specific family group. This meant He could only understand the tongue of that particular group. Remember I said that the different skin pigments of a group of people represented that group's spiritual gift. Well, now that the language of pride has been cast down, a man can only understand the language of another person that shares that particular gift.

This also makes it impossible for Satan to use the gifts of men as one unified body for himself. But most importantly it also makes it impossible for Satan to use these gifts against the One who gave man these spiritual gifts.

The only way for man to connect with gifts of the next group or nationality like they had before Babel is not to exalt themselves through pride, but to humble themselves and exalt the name of the Lord through PRAISE. For he who humbles himself shall be exalted. Praise is the common tongue that will reunite the different colors or gifts of my light. I desire to abide in the praises of my people.

If I am lifted from the earth, I will draw all men unto me. As I reveal these secrets of my Kingdom you will see that I am building my own tower. The name of it shall be high above every name.

THE FIRE OF TRUTH

The Holy Spirit plainly described Hell for me. His explanation made me realize why a loving, true, and just God could ever let anyone burn in a partially decayed state forever and never burn up. The Word of God describes it as a place of purgatory where the worm never dies and the smell of cooking flesh is like burning sulfur, choking out all of the oxygen. So not only will one be irritated by the heat of the flame, but they will choke for air. He explained His Truth as a fire that is JUST, meaning it is always the same. This means the truth is an eternal burning fire that never weakens.

The consistent eternal burning of this fire is the core of God's unchanging, undying constitution that makes up I AM, the God that doesn't change. Now the way The Holy Spirit explained this to me is that when we are transfigured and receive our glorified bodies these bodies will be the same bodies Adam and Eve had before they ate the fruit. The word of God says that man was made in the image and likeness of God. This means that the fire of Truth girded Adams and his wife's loins. The fire covers their flesh like our clothes cover us today. This fire didn't burn Adam and his wife's flesh because their flesh had not yet been corrupted by sin. Adam had the fire of truth burning within the core of his spirit. Like God, Adam's three-part being was in perfect harmony which allowed the fire of Truth that was burning within his heart to be immediately manifested on the outside of his physical body. What happens in the Spirit is manifested in the flesh. However, Adam's flesh, like his Spirit, wasn't corrupted. Adam's flesh didn't burn because it was a pure reflection of the truth that lived inside it. His flesh could live for eternity along with the Spirit. This means that Adam's flesh was on one accord with his Soul and Spirit down to the very core of his existence where the Holy Fire of God's Truth resided. Adam and Eve's flesh could live forever just like The Father, Son, and The Holy Ghost because the Soul, Spirit, and Body of Adam were on one accord.

God's Truth never contradicts or comes into conflict with itself. However, when man became corrupted through sin, the fire of truth was replaced with a lie. That lie sowed discord and separated man's spirit from his body. The result would ultimately result in a physical death because now the fleshly body couldn't get the eternal nutrients it needed from man's Spirit that allowed it to remain immortal. After the flesh was divided from the Spirit, the very substance called flesh that was meant to magnify and Glorify the fire of God's Truth now became irritated by it. The flesh couldn't even come close to the Truth anymore because it would be consumed by the very fire that once was its covering and protection.

As a result the flesh now came into conflict with the very fire that it edified to reflect the luminance of that fire upon God as a form of praise and a sign of man's obedience to God. Adam's flesh that once wore the fire of truth began to shade out God's light of truth by lifting its own opinion in front of God's light. This was the same thing that man's new father Satan did in Heaven. When the lie of Satan made man form a conflicting opinion with God's Fire of Truth, that same fire for man went from being a comforting, protecting covering to being an irritable, uncomfortable danger. As a consequence, man has placed himself in a disposition against God instead of being in a position of humility before God.

Now because of Adam, the whole Earth burns like Adam's flesh that was made from the Earth. God cursed the ground like Adam. So now like Adam, the earth has become prideful and stubborn, producing thorns and thistles. Man is the soul of the earth, which means man's body was the earth's only link to God. After Adam's flesh was separated from his Spirit which linked man to God, the earth was cut off from God as well. God created Adam in this manner so that as Adam's flesh obeyed his spirit in this same manner earth would obey Adam. Isaiah 55:12-13 KJV the prophet Isaiah tells us exactly how obedient the earth was to Adam.

Isaiah55:12-13 KJV
For ye shall go out with joy, and be led forth with peace: the mountains and the hills shall break forth before you into singing, and all the trees of the field shall clap their hands.

13Instead of the thorn shall come up the fir tree, and instead of the brier shall come up the myrtle tree: and it shall be to the LORD for a name, for an everlasting sign that shall not be cut off.

This implies in Isaiah that the earth and hills broke forth before Adam in a form of praise in the same manner that his wife Eve would in consummation which is a direct form of praise or submission. In other words, Adam didn't even have to till the soil to plant seeds, because the earth itself gladly opened up for him.

Before sin, the earth brought forth fir trees which are a symbol of **honesty**, truth, and forthrightness because of the way it grows on the "straight and narrow." The trunk of the fir reminds us of a tall straight pillar of **strength**, symbolic of the tower of truth. The earth also brought forth the myrtle tree, which is the Hebrew symbol for marriage and love. This myrtle tree was a sign to Adam that the earth loved him and it had his best interest at heart. Adam gave the seed to the earth to produce. This is why when the second Adam arrived, we can see by this scripture that it really was a Joy to the World that the Lord had come. Now once again the Earth could receive Her King; she opened the soils of her heart and prepared a room for Adam's seed…now Heaven and Nature could truly sing. The earth was on one accord with Adam like his Soul, Spirit, and Body joined within the bounds of marriage until the day Adam rebelled. After sin, the great divorce took place and earth became cursed like Adam's body producing thorns and thistles for man.

God, through Jesus, gave us the seed of life but the stubborn soils of man's sinful opinionated mind produced thorns and thistles choking that seed out. Men placed those same thorns as a crown on Jesus's head, representing our stubborn minds unwillingness to submit to an all-loving God. God's bond is so tight with his creation that He too had to suffer the pain of death so his creation could be resurrected and redeemed back to life through his Son's resurrection.

Sin placed the flesh of men and everything that is connected to it on this earth at a position that is against God's Fire of Truth. Whatever is not positioned with the Fire of Truth gets consumed. This is a set principle that has been established by God and that principle is that anytime you come into conflict with God's TRUTH…you BURN. This principle of God is true in Heaven and the earth. Heaven and earth shall pass, but my WORDS or My Truth will never fade. This is true even of Satan in Ezekiel 28 KJV where the Word of God speaks of Satan as the King of Tyre. It also speaks of Satan's destruction as a fire that will start in the midst of Satan's heart where Satan's pride, which conflicted with God's Truth, began.

Ezekiel 28 NIV

12 "Son of man, take up a lament concerning the king of Tyre and say to him: 'This is what the Sovereign Lord says:
"'You were the seal of perfection,

full of wisdom and perfect in beauty.
¹³ You were in Eden,
the garden of God;
every precious stone adorned you:
carnelian, chrysolite and emerald,
topaz, onyx and jasper,
lapis lazuli, turquoise and beryl.
Your settings and mountings were made of gold;
on the day you were created they were prepared.
¹⁴ You were anointed as a guardian cherub,
for so I ordained you.
You were on the holy mount of God;
you walked among the fiery stones.
¹⁵ You were blameless in your ways
from the day you were created
till wickedness was found in you.
¹⁶ Through your widespread trade
you were filled with violence,
and you sinned.
So I drove you in disgrace from the mount of God,
and I expelled you, guardian cherub,
from among the fiery stones.
¹⁷ Your heart became proud
on account of your beauty,
and you corrupted your wisdom
because of your splendor.
So I threw you to the earth;
I made a spectacle of you before kings.
¹⁸ By your many sins and dishonest trade
you have desecrated your sanctuaries.
So I made a fire come out from you,
and it consumed you,
and I reduced you to ashes on the ground

in the sight of all who were watching.
¹⁹ All the nations who knew you
are appalled at you;
you have come to a horrible end
and will be no more!'

It will be the fire of TRUTH that God cleanses and Purifies the world with the second time. God made a covenant with Noah by placing his rainbow in the sky. It was the first time after the fall of man in the Garden of Eden that God Birthed His covenant with man by cleansing the earth with water. This represents physical birth. The inhabitants of the earth, which was man and all the animals, were birthed into the new covenant through his son Jesus, which the Ark represents. Noah's Ark represents the Ark of the Covenant, which was carried by the priest like the floodwaters carried the Ark. Inside the ark was a covenant, or a seed, that represents a tenth of all the living land-dwelling animals in the Earth including a tenth of all mankind represented by Noah and his family. The floodwaters represent Jesus our Priest who carried the Ark over the flood while taking on all the sins of the world and dying with them. Jesus carried the seed, or the ark until it was time for the water to break and the seed to be birthed into the newly cleansed earth.

Noah's Ark, like the Ark of the Covenant, carried the seed of God until it was time for the stone tablets to be made flesh. The stone tablets are made flesh theough Jesus, the Perfect Man, born unto the Virgin Mary. The contents of the Ark of the Covenant became accessible to all men through the death of Jesus when He died for the sins of the World.

First, the rain stopped which was symbolic of Jesus' death. Second the sun symbolic of the Holy Spirit illuminated the waters. In this same manner, the Holy Spirit engulfed Jesus' body raising Him from the dead. Jesus being raised from the dead is represented by the waters being evaporated by the sunlight into the air. These waters also represent the embryonic fluid of a woman breaking so her baby can be born. The newborn baby in this case was every person and living thing in the Ark. The Ark's door was symbolic of the veil in the temple. The veil was torn in the Temple that separated God and man so that we can boldly come before God's Throne. The veil being torn represents us being born again into God's Kingdom, which is the realm of the Holy Spirit. The Ark door being opened represents Noah and all of creation being birthed from the realm of the Father into the realm of the Son. The water subsided and the sun began to shine; the evaporating water represented Jesus' resurrection from the dead and ascending to Heaven to sit at the right hand of His Father. As the sun shone bright upon the earth the first thing Noah saw as they stepped out of the ark was the FATHER'S promise for earth and man to be purified and born of Fire the next time. This represents the spiritual Birth of the HOLY SPIRIT through Fire represented by the Rainbow. So God's fire of Truth, which is the Holy Spirit, will burn sin and purify the earth. Man will also be transfigured and made pure by the fire of the Holy Spirit that his flesh becomes transparent to magnify the Light of the Lord within him. This light will be seen throughout man's being and He will look like Jesus did when He was on the Mountain of Transfiguration with the Saints.

So how does all of this have anything to do with Hell? It has everything to do with Hell because the rainbow represents the Holy Spirit and Fire. This is the same Fire of Truth that will glorify the Truth and everything that coincides with it, and at the same time burn and destroy everything that is conflicting.

That fire of Truth is the same yesterday, today, and forever. It's a personal choice if one wants to flow with it or kick against it. God doesn't destroy you by sending you to Hell. You destroy yourself by refusing to let this Truth or God's mind be in you. What burns in hell is the sin and corruption that has become a part of your makeup. Now, because you are part God and part Satan, you will never die but burn always.

Just like Satan, you originated in God but like Satan, because you chose to not have the mind of Christ and form your own opinions about God, the good in you has to now suffer with the bad. That's why the Bible says if your right hand offends or comes into conflict with my truth, it's better to cut it off and let it burn by itself than for you to be taken down in the flames of truth with it.

Matthew 5:30 CSB
30 And if your right hand causes you to sin, cut it off and throw it away. For it is better that you lose one of the parts of your body than for your whole body to go into hell.

Jesus wasn't literally talking about the cutting off of your physical hand. He was talking about casting down that thought before it causes your whole body to fall into sin. In other words, nip the conflict in the bud before your whole body comes into conflict with the truth because just a little leaven leavens the whole lump. We must learn to ignore sin as a form of resistance like God. It hurts for someone you have known your whole life to just ignore you like you never existed to them. Truth is, God gave us this tool to use against Satan's temptations, not against people. We use this tool against sin because now as a Christian you ignore the things that you use to do like they never even existed. The word of God worded it like this:

2Cor 5:17 KJV2000
Therefore if any man be in Christ, he is a new creation: old things are passed away; behold, all things are become new.

For God to ignore you as if you never existed, simply means that you never existed. God knew you or thought you into existence like Adam knew his wife and a child was birthed into existence. Every perfect will or plan for your existence was thought out before the foundations of the world. If you don't submit to his perfect will or if you don't accept his son Jesus, God will ignore you.

If you don't abide in Him and let His Spirit abide in you, God will not know you on the Day of Judgement. To put it plainly, if God cannot find any evidence of His Truth which is his son in you it will be like he never knew or begat you. It's this way because God only knows the BELIEVERS who have confessed Christ and have been reborn into His Kingdom of Heaven. Yes, he knew you before you were born, but your spirit man left his Fire of Truth where it originated, to be born into a corrupted fleshy body of sin, where it became shaded from God's Fire by your flesh. After you accepted his Son Jesus, you were born again.

This means that after you were born into His Kingdom of Righteousness, the Light of His Spirit of Truth began to shine upon you. He remembered what he had in mind for your spirit when he first thought you into existence and He renames you according to that purpose. Then and then only is when He begins to form a relationship with you.

When you were reborn into His Kingdom as a Child, he called you his beloved son and in you, He is well pleased. From that moment, the Holy Spirit began raising you in the Kingdom of Heaven like a newborn baby. As a child, you didn't bring any of your thoughts and opinions that you had in Satan's Kingdom to stand in front of God's knowledge in His Kingdom. Instead, you start from scratch by willingly and submissively letting the Holy Spirit reteach you about everything there is to know according to the truth of his Word. In you, the truth will not burn, but rather magnify or Glorify His Truth. Once again God gave us the ability to Ignore because He knew that man would need this ability to ignore the Tree of Knowledge in the Garden. Instead of using it to ignore temptation man uses it to ignore God. Look at how the dictionary defines the word ignore and then we will see exactly how man does God.

Ignore: fail to consider (something significant).

When we ignore God, we fail to consider him as being significant in our lives. In other words, He doesn't even exist. Even though God thought you into existence, if His truth is not found in you, He will ignore you like you never existed because God can only recognize His Truth. So, just like he never knew sin and if you are living in the Kingdom of Sin this simply means He never knew you as a son in his Heavenly Kingdom.

It's not this earthly Kingdom that God is saying that He never knew you in but it's the Kingdom of Heaven that He has no recollection of you being born into. When God says, "Depart from me, I never knew you." What God is actually saying, "I never knew you personally." God the Father and God the Son are Omnipresent. You can either live in Truth and let its fire protect you or you can choose to be a naked slave to sin and uplifted in pride and let the Fire of Truth consume you. It was your choice, not God's. In the end, Satan will be let out of Prison and began deceiving the nations once again but this time the Fire of Truth or the Holy Spirit will fall and consume them. Then Hell and all that were in sin, including Satan and his demons, will be thrown into the lake of fire.

Rev 20:7-10 BSB

When the thousand years are complete, Satan will be released from his prison, 8, and will go out to deceive the nations in the four corners of the earth, Gog and Magog, to assemble them for battle. Their number is like the sand of the seashore.

9 And they marched across the broad expanse of the earth and surrounded the camp of the saints and the beloved city. But fire came down from heaven and consumed them. 10 And the devil who had deceived them was thrown into the lake of fire and sulfur, into which the beast and the false prophet had already been thrown. There they will be tormented day and night forever and ever

---

THE RAINBOW OF SPIRITUAL GIFTS

Before we go any further you need to understand that God always works in a threefold manner: first the Father, then the Son, and the Holy Spirit. This is the order of God and it is reflected in everything He created. The model of this threefold principle in God's plan of Reconciliation is actually a re-creation of man into a glorified being through three realms. The first realm being the Father, the second is the realm of the Son, and the third and final is the realm of the Holy Spirit. The rainbow must be understood in this manner otherwise the acts of God which it symbolizes can be very confusing and often contradictory. I must also point out that the rainbow represents the Sevenfold Spirit that is layered upon itself to form not one, but three sevens. These three sevens come together in a perfect alliance to form one being and His mark is SEVEN SEVEN SEVEN.

The Rainbow, which represents the sevenfold spirit, must be understood in three parallel layers and that these parallel layers are infinite like God. We will also have to understand that it would be impossible to write a book explaining all the symbolic meanings and parallels in their entirety because God is inexhaustible.

The Rainbow is the Promise of God to mankind that He would no longer baptize or destroy the world through death and wash sin away by water. The Rainbow represents the realm of Fire where the Truth will be made known to all men. Instead, He would consume sin by burning it and purifying the world once and for all with the Holy Ghost and fire. I use the word baptism because it represents death, but a death that is not permanent. Baptism is the perfect word to describe how we as Believers only die once but we will be resurrected to live always.

When Jesus said I will tear down or destroy this temple and rebuild it in three days. He was speaking of His Death, burial, and resurrection. Death is always the end of a way of life in a particular realm. In Noah's ark, death is represented by the waters that covered man like the dirt covers the grave. The waters also represent the washing away of man's sin by the water of the word. As previously stated when man came out of the ark, He was birthed into a new realm represented by the door of the ark opening and birthing a tenth or a seed of creation from the realm of God the Father into the Realm of God the Son. Then shortly after man had been baptized represented by man coming out of the ark, God then sent the promise of the Holy Spirit in the form of a Rainbow.

The Rainbow means that even though man had just been birthed into the realm of the Son with water, it was God's plan to eventually birth man into the realm of the Holy Spirit with fire. The seven visible colors of the rainbow give it away because the number seven is the number of The Holy Spirit.

The number seven is a combination of two sets of numbers plus one. The first set is three which is always perfection because three represents completion and divinity of the Father, Son, and Holy Spirit as one God. The next set of three also represents perfection because Man was made in the image and likeness of God. These two numerals added together give you sum total of six, which is also the number of man. Then if you add the number one to that you will get seven, which is God with man, representing the Holy Spirit. The Church is the physical manifestation of the reunion of God and man. Remember that man was once united with God in the Garden of Eden, but Adam divorced God through sin, so God sent his Holy Spirit to be reunited with man.

Revelation 3 Living Bible (TLB)
3 "To the leader of the church in Sardis write this letter:
"This message is sent to you by the one who has the sevenfold Spirit of God and the seven stars.

After the Baptism of Christ, the Holy Spirit descends upon Him in the form of a Dove, just as He does when we confess that Jesus is our Lord and Savior. This reunion of God and man is how God desires to empower man so that he could be victoriously birthed into the realm of fire which is the realm of the Holy Spirit. After you are rebirthed, the Holy Spirit descends or comes into you like when He first breathed himself into Adam. Creation was the realm of God the Father who walked and talked with Adam to teach him. Jesus said that you must enter the kingdom as a child. This means as you grow in Christ, by being taught the word through hearing and reading, you then become mature in Christ. Maturity is where you can hear and know the voice of the Holy Spirit as He imparts deeper knowledge of the scriptures. This is how the Father reveals his plans and purposes for our lives like he did for Adam.

Baptism is a way to physically represent how we gave up our old sinful ways and now have come forth rebirthed into the Kingdom of Heaven where God in the form of the Holy Spirit can once again talk with man.

Noah entered The Realm of Water. The water represents the fleshly Body of Jesus so we will now refer to Jesus as being The Water of The Word of God. The Water of the Word of God took on all the weight of all of the corrupted things which includes mankind, animals, and plants, and then defeated sin by drowning it out. The dark cloud covering the sun represents God the Father turning his face away from Jesus.

Noah and his family in the ark represent two things: one is the dead believers resting in the bosom of Abraham and the other is the remnant of BELIEVERS taken up in the rapture. The ark represents God's covenant with man. Finally, the Father turns his Sun or his face back upon the waters representing Easter morning and the waters receded representing the resurrection of Jesus. Then Noah confides in a Dove to let him know when to open the door of the Ark. This represents our present time where Jesus is no longer with us in the flesh so we have to rely on faith in His Holy Spirit to guide us into all truth. The dove representing the Holy Spirit brings back an olive branch representing the anointing. The anointing breaks the yoke represented by the sealed door of the ark. After the anointing breaks the seal the door opens allowing Noah, his family, and all the animals to be birthed into a new earth or a new realm in God. This new realm is called the realm of baptism or the realm of the Son. The realm of the Son comes with the promise of the Holy Spirit who will carry us into the next realm which is the realm of fire.

Matthew 3:11NIV
"I baptize you with water for repentance. But after me comes one who is more powerful than I, whose sandals I am not worthy to carry. He will baptize you with the Holy Spirit and fire."

Here John plays the same role as God the Father did way back during the flood of Noah by baptizing Jesus in Matthew's account of the Gospel. John the Baptist reveals the Father's mighty plan of reaping the world back to himself by taking it back from Satan. Men are the wheat and Jesus came to cut them away from their roots in Satan and gather them like wheat (or the souls of mankind) and bind them and their gifts back together again for His Father. John the Baptist baptized men with water just like the Father baptized and cleansed the world by washing it free of sin with the Water of the Word which is the Word of God. Now in that same manner, as God provided His son Jesus or the Water of THE WORD for cleansing and repentance, Jesus will provide the Holy Spirit who will purify us and the earth to the point that we won't have the will to sin anymore by baptizing us in the Fire of Truth.

Ephesians 5:26 King James 2000 Bible
That he might sanctify and cleanse it with the washing
of water by the word

The Water of the Word came to cleanse us daily from our sins and the Fire of the Holy Spirit came to purify us so that we will never sin again. The Rainbow promises total purification by fire from our sins.

The Rainbow represents the Holy Spirit, plus the other six visible colors representing the original six different groups of families on the earth, plus God. Man was separated from God until Jesus' death, burial, and resurrection. The Rainbow was a promise to Noah that God would dwell on the earth with man once again when the time was right. The rainbow presents seven layers or seven folds representing Jerusalem which will eventually be the New Jerusalem. The New Jerusalem will descend to earth as a physical manifestation of what the church represents to man today and that is God on Earth. Just like the Garden of Eden, Jerusalem will be the central governing nation of The New Earth governing the other six nations.

This means when you look at the rainbow, it represents the six nations plus the Nation of Jerusalem which is the seventh nation. Jesus will sit on the throne in Jerusalem where the crown of government will rest upon His' shoulders and He will rule the seven continents and have dominion over the seven seas that are represented by the seven churches or the council chambers before his throne room. Now there are other colors of the rainbow but there are only seven that are visible to the naked eye. These colors represent God and man, but they also represent the different seven Gifts of the Holy Spirit.

As I stated before the color of the skin of your particular nationality or family group reflects the main gift of your family group. The variations of colors stemming out from that main gift represent the variations of gifts within that particular family. This can be seen on the rainbow as the main color fades into the next main color.

These Gifts magnify and reflect the light of Truth with the brilliance of that gift back upon the throne of God. The origination of the (I) and the (M) that form the prefix IM in the word IM-AGE has its roots in the name I AM. I AM is who God said that He was when Moses asked Him for His name. IM-AGE or Image literally means to reflect on to God. Adam was made in the image and likeness of God, which meant that he was a perfect reflection of God just like Jesus.

This is why Jesus said if you have seen me you have also seen the Father. This is the reason why Jesus is also called the second Adam. The only thing that Jesus has that Adam didn't is his Father's blood flowing through him. This blood from His Father carried the cannot sin DNA trait. Jesus was flesh so that he could be tempted like his mother Mary, but he didn't have the ability to give in to that temptation because he carried the cannot sin blood DNA trait of His Father God. God knew that Jesus could only respond to sin in the same manner that He would because Jesus was His biological Son born in HIS IMAGE and LIKENESS, unlike Adam who was just created in His IMAGE and LIKENESS.

This IMAGE of God is represented by the air and Jesus is represented by the water molecules in the air. The evaporated water molecules represent the Son being taken up into the air, which also represents Jesus's ascension from earth to Heaven. Air represents the UNSEEN FATHER GOD because air has never been seen by man and no man has seen the Father.

Even now that Jesus is unseen, he has sent His Spirit in order to fulfill his promise that He would be with us always even unto the end of the world. He has given us the Light of His Holy Spirit to shine upon His Truth which was hidden from us like the evaporated water molecules.

This is made possible because of the Light of the Holy Spirit reflecting off of the invisible evaporated water molecules that also represent Jesus's unseen fleshly body. What we see because of all this happening in the spiritual realm is the physical manifestation of a rainbow in this natural realm.

Daniel 2:22 New American Standard Bible
"It is He who reveals the profound and hidden things;
He knows what is in the darkness, And the light dwells
with Him.

John 14:9-10 NIV
Jesus answered: "Don't you know me, Philip, even af-
ter I have been among you such a long time? Anyone
who has seen me has seen the Father. How can you say,
'Show us the Father'? 10Don't you believe that I am in
the Father, and that the Father is in me? The words I say
to you I do not speak on my own authority. Rather, it is
the Father, living in me, who is doing his work.

Every little piece fits together like a puzzle. Now we understand why we as the Body of Christ must reflect that same Light of the Holy Spirit before all men so they may see our good works and glorify our Father in Heaven.

In the water molecule, you have two hydrogen and one oxygen molecule which are invisible gases that come together to create a visible liquid. Like Jesus, water is the embodiment of all three gases. Even though the two hydrogen molecules are the same, I like to think of one hydrogen molecule as the Son and the other hydrogen as the Holy Spirit. This visible substance called water represents Jesus perfectly because, like water, Jesus is the physical visible embodiment of all three separate deities. Now we have a deeper meaning of what was actually happening in John Chapter 1 because we realize that the water in Genesis and the Word were one and the same as the two hydrogen molecules that make up water. In Genesis, we learn that the water that covered the whole Earth was the physical embodiment of the Word of God in John Chapter 1. Later on, we learn that the Word of God in the physical form of water along with the Holy Spirit of God, moved upon the waters like He did Adam. All forms of life can find their origin in water. Water was here on earth before anything else ever was.

The Apostle John however was told by the Holy Spirit that it wouldn't be any water on the new earth except for the four rivers. Why? In John Chapter 1, it said the Word was made flesh and dwelt among men. So, if the Word that was in the form of water, in the beginning, was made flesh, then why would there be any need for water? The Word that was known as the floodwaters in Genesis became a fleshly man that we now know as Jesus. Jesus took upon himself all the sins of the world and died erasing our sins as the water did at the flood of Noah. When Jesus ascended to Heaven, the Father sent the Holy Spirit as promised. This is what the rainbow represents: the promise of the Holy Spirit that came after the water had evaporated or after Jesus ascended to heaven. The water being evaporated means that this era of water will pass, as our former bodies, and be made new.

Remember the life source that we came from; we have to continually be connected to in order to live. We were made from clay which originated from water, so we constantly need water to replenish ourselves. Clay without water will soon dry out and therefore we thirst for it regularly.

We use water to refresh our bodies and water is a representation of Jesus's fleshly Body. God the Father gave us his son Jesus, who is now our living spiritual life-sustaining water. Now through Jesus, our spirits have been made righteous but still resides within our sin-cursed flesh. Jesus died for us so that we could continually wash away our sins by eating and drinking the bread and water of His Word.

John 4:7-14 NIV

7 When a Samaritan woman came to draw water, Jesus said to her, "Will you give me a drink?" 8 (His disciples had gone into the town to buy food.)

9 The Samaritan woman said to him, "You are a Jew and I am a Samaritan woman. How can you ask me for a drink?" (For Jews do not associate with Samaritans. [a])

10 Jesus answered her, "If you knew THE GIFT of God and who it is that asks you for a drink, you would have asked him and he would have given you living water."

11 "Sir," the woman said, "you have nothing to draw with and the well is deep. Where can you get this living water? 12 Are you greater than our father Jacob, who gave us the well and drank from it himself, as did also his sons and his livestock?"

13 Jesus answered, "Everyone who drinks this water will be thirsty again, 14 but whoever drinks the water I give them will never thirst. Indeed, the water I give them will become in them a spring of water welling up to eternal life."

By reading this passage, can you tell where the water went that John spoke about in Rev 21 that was represented by Jesus? Jesus was the gift of water that represents the Word who was present at the well with the woman. She didn't realize that Jesus was that very Gift of water that she needed to sustain her. She drew Jesus to her by her thirst. Then, as she drew from the well of the natural water, the living water who was Jesus, began to minister to her. It is no coincidence that both the natural and the living water could be found in the same place because the natural is a direct manifestation of the spiritual.

The Samaritan woman's natural thirst kept her coming back to this well for hydration but her spirit was still thirsty and dried out by her many sins. The unsatisfied state of the Samaritan woman was represented by her past husband's and the sinful adulterous relationship that she was currently involved in at the time. Jesus let the woman know *that this water can't be drawn with a bucket but hearing and believing me is the only way to drink the Living Water.* As you believe or drink of me, repent and let the living water fill the vast dry river bed of your heart. The Gift of Living Water that you thirst for will be on the inside of you welling up and running over into eternal life. This constant flowing well now represents the endless, life-sustaining knowledge of God. What the woman lacked, she now had an abundance of to the point that rivers of living water flowed out from her. So where are the waters of the sea in the Era of the Rainbow? Those waters will be inside us because the water of the word will become a part of us, reflecting the Glorious light of the Holy Spirit just as the water molecules in the air form a rainbow. We know that this rainbow represents Jesus who was on earth but now has evaporated and ascended to be with His Father in Heaven.

In the era of the Holy Spirit, just like the body of Jesus which has become unseen, the bodies of water will have become unseen as well. The oceans represent an era when we had to wash away sin by the covering of water representing death. The sins of the children of God were covered by the death of an animal and consumed by fire. The waters used to wash the altar represent the renewal of our minds with the Word of God. The Gift, as Jesus calls himself, died for our sins so that we wouldn't have to go through this ritual process of cleansing in its physical form. Jesus became the sacrificial Lamb who died after taking on all of our sins as the floodwaters did to sinful people in Noah's day. Then Jesus took our many sins to hell to burn. The fire that burned the animals' carcasses that had now been laden with the sins of the person who offered it up for sacrifice, represented Hell's fire. The last thing would be the renewal of our minds through the washing of the water by the WORD. The priest washing the altars represents our Clergy ministering the Word to us. Now that we understand that Jesus represents all three of these things through water, we can also understand that after we are transfigured, there will be no need for cleansing by washing with water. The first reason is that a sinless man has no reason to repent or to be cleansed. The second reason will be because we will no longer have created flesh like that of Adams which has to be washed daily of our sins. We will no longer have to be covered by the law of adoption that makes us sons of God, but we will be born of the Holy Spirit and Fire and changed into biological sons through birth. So that same blood of the lamb and water of Word that was used to cover us and to make us pure will become a part of our genetic make-up. Once you drink the living water, it will become a part of you to the point that you will constantly be replenished by it in the same way that your blood now currently renews your natural body. This process of constant renewal will be so efficient that you will live forever and never thirst for temporal earthly sustainment again.

We have to be purified from the inside out because it's not what enters a man that corrupts him, but what comes out of him in the form of his words and deeds that defile him.

Mark 7:20-23 NIV
20And then he added, "It is what comes from inside that defiles you. 21For from within, out of a person's heart, come evil thoughts, sexual immorality, theft, murder, 22adultery, greed, wickedness, deceit, lustful desires, envy, slander, pride, and foolishness. 23All these vile things come from within; they are what defile you."

The Realm of the Holy Spirit is the realm of fire that begets light in the form of Wisdom, Knowledge, and Understanding. The fire of the Holy Ghost also creates heat for purification and protection. Light and heat are both products of fire.

Isaiah 4:2-4 TLB
2-4 Those whose names are written down to escape the destruction of Jerusalem will be washed and rinsed of all their moral filth by the horrors and the fire.

Isaiah speaks of fire used to wash and rinse in the realm of the Spirit like water was used in the realm of the Body. Isaiah also speaks of the daughters of Zion referring to the seven churches of the seven groups of people that were spread abroad. In the Old Testament Isaiah foretells how the churches will be cleansed first of fire. The Church represents the mindset of a particular group of people. God always starts at the center, representing the Garden of Eden. His ultimate goal is to be the center of every man's attention.

Isaiah 9:8 NIV
8. For a child is born to us,
a son is given to us.
The government will rest on his shoulders.
And he will be called:
Wonderful Counselor, Mighty God,
Everlasting Father, Prince of Peace.
7.His government and its peace
will never end.
He will rule with fairness and justice from the throne of
his ancestor David

for all eternity.
The passionate commitment of the LORD of Heaven's
Armies
will make this happen!

The Center is the Throne room or the council chamber spoke about in Proverbs 31:23. In the New International Version, it speaks of the civic leaders as the elders of the land. These elders are the leaders of the seven land masses or the seven continents on earth. His government of peace will never end and He will run it from the pulpit. The four pillars of this platform represent what Jesus is to the Kingdom of Heaven and all mankind:

<u>Wonderful Counselor</u>
<u>Mighty God</u>
<u>Everlasting Father</u>
<u>Prince of Peace</u>

Her husband in Proverbs:31-23 is speaking of Jesus: the Government shall be on his shoulders and his virtuous wife is the body of Christ. The church is the Bride of Christ. We the Church are the children of Eve whom Jesus came to redeem. Jesus, (the second Adam) came to redeem his bride, who was our earthly mother Eve. In Eden, these would be the duties of Eve. Even now, these are the duties of her children which are the women, and men who make up the Church or the Bride of Christ. These duties are laid out in Proverbs 31.

Proverbs 31:10-31 NIV
A wife of noble character who can find?
She is worth far more than rubies.
11.Her husband has full confidence in her

and lacks nothing of value.
12.She brings him good, not harm,
all the days of her life.
13.She selects wool and flax
and works with eager hands.
14.She is like the merchant ships,
bringing her food from afar.
15.She gets up while it is still night;
she provides food for her family
and portions for her female servants.
16.She considers a field and buys it;
out of her earnings she plants a vineyard.
17.She sets about her work vigorously;
her arms are strong for her tasks.
18.She sees that her trading is profitable,
and her lamp does not go out at night.
19.In her hand she holds the distaff
and grasps the spindle with her fingers.
20.She opens her arms to the poor
and extends her hands to the needy.
21.When it snows, she has no fear for her household;
for all of them are clothed in scarlet.
22.She makes coverings for her bed;
she is clothed in fine linen and purple.
23.Her husband is respected at the city gate,
where he takes his seat among the elders of the land.
24.She makes linen garments and sells them,
and supplies the merchants with sashes.
25.She is clothed with strength and dignity;
she can laugh at the days to come.
26.She speaks with wisdom,
and faithful instruction is on her tongue.
27.She watches over the affairs of her household

and does not eat the bread of idleness.
28.Her children arise and call her blessed;
her husband also, and he praises her:
29."Many women do noble things,
but you surpass them all."
30.Charm is deceptive, and beauty is fleeting;
but a woman who fears the Lord is to be praised.
31.Honor her for all that her hands have done,
and let her works bring her praise at the city gate.

Jesus is seen by John, the beloved disciple in Revelations 3, holding up these civic leaders who are the leaders of the seven Churches represented by the seven stars. Why is Jesus holding up the leaders of the seven churches? Whatever God holds up in front of you, represents what is about to happen next. Remember how the rainbow was uplifted by God? This was God's way of telling Noah what was about to happen next. As you read through this prophetic living word of God you will see how the plan of reconciliation is foretold in many different ways and also how it was prophesied until it was actually manifested by the Birth, Death, and Resurrection of Jesus Christ, the Son of God. When you get to Revelations 2, Jesus reveals in full detail what he has already done for mankind through the different descriptions of his symbolic body. Each part of his body in this chapter represents what he has done for mankind.

Revelation 1:9-20 TLB
I am the A and the Z, the Beginning and the Ending of
all things," says God, who is the Lord, the All Powerful
*One who is, and was, and is coming again!**

9 It is I, your brother John, a fellow sufferer for the
Lord's sake, who am writing this letter to you. I, too,

have shared the patience Jesus gives, and we shall share his Kingdom!

I was on the island of Patmos, exiled there for preaching the Word of God and for telling what I knew about Jesus Christ. 10 It was the Lord's Day and I was worshiping, when suddenly I heard a loud voice behind me, a voice that sounded like a trumpet blast, 11 saying, "I am A and Z, the First and Last!" And then I heard him say, "Write down everything you see, and send your letter to the seven churches in Turkey: to the church in Ephesus, the one in Smyrna, and those in Pergamos, Thyatira, Sardis, Philadelphia, and Laodicea."

12 When I turned to see who was speaking, there behind me were seven candlesticks of gold. 13 And standing among them was one who looked like Jesus, who called himself the Son of Man, wearing a long robe circled with a golden band across his chest. 14 His hair was white as wool or snow, [h] and his eyes penetrated like flames of fire. 15 His feet gleamed like burnished bronze, and his voice thundered like the waves against the shore. 16 He held seven stars in his right hand and a sharp, double-bladed sword in his mouth, and his face shone like the power of the sun in unclouded brilliance.

17-18 When I saw him, I fell at his feet as dead; but he laid his right hand on me and said, "Don't be afraid! Though I am the First and Last, the Living One who died, who is now alive forevermore, who has the keys of hell and death—don't be afraid! 19 Write down what you have just seen and what will soon be shown to you. 20 This is the meaning of the seven stars you saw in my right hand and the seven golden candlesticks: The seven stars are the leaders of the seven churches, and the seven candlesticks are the churches themselves.

After He showed John everything He had done for mankind, He held up the rainbow representing the seven stars and the heads of the 7 churches. By doing this, God is telling us He is going to judge and purify the mind of the church which are the leaders first and then the church as a body next.

The purification of man in the Era of the rainbow leading up to the end of time and the beginning of eternity is the beginning of the unseen realm for man. This realm is all about God's likeness being reflected by man. Man magnifies the Light while reflecting it back upon God. We were created for HIS Glory to reflect the light of God back upon Him just like a rainbow. We have to be in total submission, so we will be totally transparent before God like a water molecule in the air. Just as the rainbow is a beautiful sign representing God, we shall be a perfect sign of the purified, sinless, glorified body of man. The visible colors of the rainbow only represents man who is a reflection of God's spirit in the earth. But where the rainbow meets the earth represents the realm that we can't see as mere men with fleshly bodies that are sinful and corrupt. The unseen part of the rainbow also represents the realm that sin-corrupted bodies cannot travel to in their current state. This is the heavenly realm. The rainbow doesn't end but forms a complete circle because it's more than just a sign in Nature.

Revelation 4 Living Bible (TLB)
4 Then as I looked, I saw a door standing open in heaven, and the same voice I had heard before, which sounded like a mighty trumpet blast, spoke to me and said, "Come up here and I will show you what must happen in the future!"

²And instantly I was in spirit there in heaven and saw—oh, the glory of it!—a throne and someone sitting on it! ³ Great bursts of light flashed forth from him as from a glittering diamond or from a shining ruby, and a RAINBOW glowing like an emerald ENCIRCLED his throne. ⁴ Twenty-four smaller thrones surrounded his, with twenty-four Elders sitting on them; all were clothed in white, with golden crowns upon their heads. ⁵ Lightning and thunder issued from the throne, and there were voices in the thunder. Directly in front of his throne were seven lighted lamps representing the sevenfold Spirit of God. ⁶ Spread out before it was a shiny crystal sea. Four Living Beings, dotted front and back with eyes, stood at the throne's four sides. ⁷ The first of these Living Beings was in the form of a lion; the second looked like an ox; the third had the face of a man; and the fourth, the form of an eagle, with wings spread out as though in flight. ⁸ Each of these Living Beings had six wings, and the central sections of their wings were covered with eyes. Day after day and night after night they kept on saying, "Holy, holy, holy, Lord God Almighty—the one who was, and is, and is to come."

⁹ And when the Living Beings gave glory and honor and thanks to the one sitting on the throne, who lives forever and ever, ¹⁰ the twenty-four Elders fell down before him and worshiped him, the Eternal Living One, and cast their crowns before the throne, singing, ¹¹ "O Lord, you are worthy to receive the glory and the honor and the power, for you have created all things. They were created and called into being by your act of will."

The rainbow that you see in the natural realm is just as colorful in the Spiritual realm which goes along with the Principle stated in Matthew 18:18.

Matthew 18:18 KJV
18Verily I say unto you, whatsoever ye shall bind on earth shall be bound in heaven: and whatsoever ye shall loose on earth shall be loosed in heaven.

This is a principle displayed by the rainbow: whatever you can see with your fleshly eyes is directly connected to that which you can't see. The unseen center of the rainbow represents the government of God and his unseen throne room. The throne room of God was the target that the seven family groups of people were aiming for before the language of Babel was confused. If you picture the rainbow as colorful rings around Saturn, these colorful rings would represent the different nationalities of mankind that reflect God's Glory back upon Him. Where the massive sphere is at the center of the rings is where God's throne room would be. In the same manner that Lucifer once encompassed God's throne room with humility and praise, the rings surround Saturn in that same manner. Saturn would be the perfect model of God's government. This circle represents the never-ending eternal life that surrounds the originator of life, the Great I AM Himself. Since man first laid eyes on the rainbow, he has observed its larger outer rings first and how its different colors of light go from the brightest to the darkest as his gaze moves toward the center of the rainbow. Sin causes man to see the outward appearance first just like one would notice and praise a runner who finishes first in a race as the winner. However, God considers and sees the center or the innermost part first. This area is called the heart. God's race is not a race to see who finishes first. His race is not given to the swift or the strong but to the one who can endure to the end, the one who can stand the weight of all the rest. Man would always look from the sinful, prideful eye and reject what seems to be the smallest; but for the one man that men wouldn't even consider, God gave him the authority to be his chief cornerstone.

For this reason, what man considers first is really last. If you look at the rainbow from God's viewpoint, the last ring on the rainbow is the one that is closest to where He sits on His throne. This makes the inner ring of the rainbow the first in God's line of sight. The innermost ring is also the darkest color of the rainbow. This darkness represents humility and this is also the color of the garment that God chooses to clothe himself with. As stated before these colors represent the category of gifts assigned to a particular nationality of mankind.

For[b] the Lord does not see as man sees; for man looks at the outward appearance, but the Lord looks at the heart."1 Samuel 16:7 NKJV

A test of humility and endurance is seen in the heart of the man that carried Jesus' cross. God has given and placed each gift according to how it pleases Him and not man. Please don't let the following secrets that were revealed to me, offend you.

Man has gone down in recorded history as having overlooked the least of these which represents Jesus because of his prideful, sinful, selfish, instinct inherited from Satan. Man has always exalted Satan's competitive nature above God's Patient Nature. We all have instinctive traits that automatically put these qualities first: the tallest, the strongest, the fastest, or the fairest in complexion, just to name a few things that identify the satanic competitive trait found in man. For this reason, man has purposely tried to eliminate his brother as Cain did with Abel to exalt himself in his brother's place. This sin trait is the competitive nature of Satan that has infiltrated man and animal alike to fight each other unto death. This will be discussed in the chapter entitled Completion over Competition. However, let us focus our attention on what we observed before and that is the man that carried Jesus' cross to Calvary was a man of dark complexion.

The dark-skinned man was looked upon as being insignificant in the eyes of most believers. However, this man copied the role of what used to be the job of Lucifer. Carrying the cross is another example of praise and servanthood, not as a slave as one may think, but of power in the same respects as a King. This man humbled himself in praise by carrying Jesus' Cross. Then he became a servant. By becoming a servant, he became a king because of the Godly principle that he who humbles himself shall be exalted. Like King David, this man was to be a King in the eyes of God because he carried the cross in front of Jesus' future believers. Jesus wants all of us to take up the cross of His cause so that His will can be manifested on the earth.

The Roman centurion selected the dark-skinned man to carry the cross because this man was the closest to Jesus in the crowd on that particular day plus the centurion considered this man as the least among the other men. In other words, the Roman soldier chose him because in his eyes the role of carrying the cross for convicted criminals was the task for slaves. Jesus was convicted and sentenced to death for our sins but not because he was sinful. What the Roman Centurion didn't know was that this man was chosen by God to do this task because whoever is the least in the eyes of men is the greatest in the eyes of God. What seemed to be only a last resort for man was God's chosen all along. When Jesus looked up, a dark-skinned man was the first man he saw after he had collapsed on the ground under the weight of the cross. Why was he so close to Jesus? Perhaps he had heard a man from Galilee was tried and convicted, then sentenced to death for crimes he didn't commit. Maybe what drew the black man from the crowd was because he could relate to His pain of being wrongfully accused, rejected, and labeled by people. What the dark-skinned man and Jesus had in common is that he was the closest to Jesus spiritually. The dark-skinned man was so close to the throne of suffrage and humility that God placed faith and confidence in him to carry the weight of the world on his shoulders for His Son's sake and endure it until it was time to do what only Jesus could do himself. Only Jesus, the Son of God, could endure the pain and shame of being nailed to a cross and raised up for all mankind to see the price for their sins. Calvary like the center of the rainbow represents the darkness of humility where God's throne room is hidden. As God looks out from the center of humility, the one He sees first represents a dark-skinned people that the scriptures mention last. The scriptures tell us that the last shall be first, and the first shall be last.

The era of the rainbow or of the Seven-Fold Spirit will be led by the dark-skinned man. The stone that the builders of the church rejected will become the chosen chief cornerstone. Everything points to the least in God's kingdom. The least shall become the greatest; the meek shall inherit the earth. These truths are not to offend the rest of the brothers in God's body. Cain was offended by God and hated his brother because God favored his brother Abel's offering.

Genesis 4:2-5 NIV. Now Abel kept flocks, and Cain worked the soil. 3 In the course of time Cain brought some of the fruits of the soil as an offering to the Lord. 4 And Abel also brought an offering—fat portions from some of the firstborn of his flock. The Lord looked with favor on Abel and his offering, 5 but on Cain and his offering he did not look with favor.

So Cain was jealous because he thought his gift didn't hold any significance in God's sight. Cain failed to realize that God placed every gift in the body just how it pleases him. Just because He looks upon a certain gift at a particular time simply means that in God's eye it's time for that particular gift to complete its specific purpose. Just as the Roman

Centurion chose the black man to carry the Cross, means God looked upon him in favor of his gift that he had to present to God at that point in history. He did a job that only he could do because it was something that only his heart could identify with and God knew that he would put his whole heart into it to get the job done. God was looking at the spiritual gift he had placed deep down in the man, where the seed of the next generation resided, representing his children who would carry on the work of carrying the cross to see if this man could reflect the image of God's Son, Jesus. In taking on this great load, He would lead his people by servanthood, through the era of the Holy Spirit, like God's son Jesus did when He was on this earth. God has chosen the black man to lead at this time according to the order in which He placed the gift given to him. Yes, the cross of Calvary was the end of the era of Sacrifice for the atonement of sin by animals. However, the unfinished work of healing the sick and raising the dead has to be taken up and carried by a people that will carry it with the same grace and humility as Jesus did. Not to discount all the rest of the gifts or brothers and sisters characterized by the different dispensation of colors of the Rainbow. All will play a role in carrying Jesus' Cross, according to the dispensation of the different gifts of the Seven-Fold Spirit.

Now that we have determined that God looks from the inside out and man from the outside in, we can see God's system is the same system that He has given to man to use. God's system of humility that looks within results in exaltation throughout. This perspective is reflected all throughout the Word of God. Everything that God created operates according to this system. This system creates unity and growth that is built upon a strong core or foundation. There are many examples, but we will look at only three.

One is the seed and how it starts in the center and grows. You can also see it from Abraham's perspective when God tells him He will give to him everything his eye could see and multiply his seed like the sand on the seashore. Abraham was on the inside looking out, representing meekness, humility, and unselfishness. Another example is when God imparted Knowledge into the heart of the Apostle Simon about Jesus. After Jesus recognized the Gift that His Father had placed on Simon, he changed his name to Peter. This represents that which was within Peter has now made room for him and is manifest as the Church throughout. Jesus says on this GIFT or ROCK of revelation, I will build my church. Your Gift is the foundation that God gave to you and on that gift, He will build everything else in your life, according to how it pleases him and the gates of Hell will not prevail against it. This same principle held true for Simon Peter and for the black man, also named Simon, who carried Jesus' cross and for all of us who are in the Body of Christ. With so many gifts that God has given man through his Holy Spirit, it's no wonder the rainbow is so colorful and the different shaded humans all reflect his light in a different way. This makes it unique to God's creation and in perfect accordance with his Divine order. The treasure is found at the heart center of the rainbow because the rainbow is a complete circle that is eternal and never-ending just like the Seven-Fold Spirit it represents. Where a man's treasure is his heart is also.

Revelation 4:2-3 TLB [2] And instantly I was in spirit there in heaven and saw—oh, the glory of it!— a throne and someone sitting on it! [3] Great bursts of light flashed forth from him as from a glittering diamond or from a shining ruby, and a rainbow glowing like an emerald encircled his throne.

A Call to Order

Joseph is represented by the Onyx stone. The Spiritual energy of this stone represents suffering, He himself is the sufferer. Everything that Joseph is and how he is presented to the world all the way down to when he was born, represents mankind in general. All of mankind has experienced suffering, but he also represents a group of people. His stone color gives him away as the darkest and one of the most ancient gemstones ever recorded on earth. This stone goes all the way back to Eden as one of the first stones mentioned in Genesis. Archeologists have found that the essence of this stone is found in Africa and Geneticists have also stated that Africa is the Essence of humanity. This leads scientists down a Biblical road to a people in which the word of God lines up with not only the lineage of Joseph linking them to Joseph's great grandfather Abraham by law but also Joseph's life experiences. Joseph stands for a people of a very dark complexion that represent endurance and the lessons that it teaches. Darkness, or blackness, is the essence of all colors and it's where the creator chooses to reside. Yes, Darkness is what God chooses to cloth himself in to display all power by enshrouding it with the robe of humility.

Psalms18:11 NLT He shrouded himself in darkness.

Only God would choose to hide the brilliant light of all power behind the dark garment of humility. However, this dark garment's true colors are seen in their true light when they are displayed on Joseph in Genesis who wore this very robe. Here Joseph is seen wearing the same robe in the natural realm that God wears in the supernatural. In the natural realm, this robe displayed all the colors of the rainbow unseen in the spiritual realm. The many different colors of Joseph's coat correlated with the rainbow of gifts and signified that he was very gifted. This was a part of God's perfect design because, in Joseph's early life, he was a little prideful. Who wouldn't be? He walked around in a very colorful coat representing the fact that he was multi-talented and highly favored by his father far above all his brothers. Joseph was lifted in pride because of the many gifts that his father had blessed him with. God had also shown him in a dream that he would be honored above the rest of his brothers with pride Joseph told this dream to his parents and siblings, which made his brothers hate him. His father Jacob said, "son do you actually expect me your mother, and your brothers to bow before you?" Born into the prideful traits of Satan one can't blame Joseph for acting in this manner. Speaking of Satan who once wore his many gifts as colorful gemstones rose up in pride as well. Lucifer like Joseph flaunted the many gifts given to him by God before the other angels of heaven as Joseph proudly wore the colorful coat that his father made him. . Josephs' pride was according to God's Devine process. God used Joseph's life to symbolize what dark-skinned people must endure to live out Joseph's dream. Joseph's life is also a roadmap for his brothers that symbolize all the other nationalities of people. This roadmap shows all members of the human race the path they must take to live out this dreamer's Dream as the favored child of his father, Joseph was hated by his brothers, and one day as Joseph approached them with a message from their father they plotted to kill him. They would've succeeded if his oldest brother Reuben hadn't pleaded for his life. It's imperative that you keep in mind that every event that happened to Joseph directly correlates with the events that led up to the enslavement and dilemma that black people currently are going through in the United States and throughout the world. It's also important that you remember Joseph's brothers represent other nationalities of people. The first in the line of succession was that his brothers stripped Joseph of his robe of many colors. Joseph's robe that represented His many gifts is how his father Jacob identified him. God orders and identifies us according to the gifts He has placed within us. By stripping Joseph of his coat his brothers had stolen his identity. Black people had their identity stolen by their brothers of other nationalities meaning they were stripped of the surname that identified them and tied them to the lineage of their fathers. Inheritance, government, and authority were also stripped away from Joseph and Black people by their brothers taking their robes. Next, Joseph was thrown into a cistern which represents that Joseph was subjected to inhumane and unsanitary treatment by his brothers while they sat down and ate. This event applies to how black people were subjected to overcrowded, inhumane, and unsanitary conditions as they were chained in the belly of slave ships that were headed to foreign countries. This brings us to the next event where Joseph's brothers profited by selling him to a caravan of merchants for twenty shekels of silver. These merchants took Joseph to Egypt. What is significant about Joseph and the black people in this event is that they both were sold for a profit to slave ship merchants under the direction of their own leaders represented by Joseph's older brothers. These merchant ships were overfilled with black families from other tribes like the twelve tribes of Israel. These ships filled with black people were headed to the United States and other parts of the world. As Joseph was being shipped to Egypt his brothers were thinking of a way to cover up what they had done. They thought up a way of disguising what they had done to Joseph by slaughtering a ram and dipping Joseph's robe in its blood. They told their father Israel that Joseph was attacked and eaten by a wild animal. The dark-shaded color of the black people now directly correlates to what was done to Joseph's coat in the hands of his brothers. Joseph's coat of bright colors was covered with blood that turned dark as the coat dried. This is symbolic of the dark coat of humility worn by God the father and the dark coat of skin worn by black people. This also signified that Joseph was made humble like God representing the suffrage of black people. This covert plan was designed in order to prevent their father Jacob from seeing the truth about what happened to his son Joseph. This represents that the black people's lineage in the Word of God would be erased from Biblical text by his brothers. Next in Joseph's plight was that He was sold to the estate of Potiphar and because of his gifts, he was quickly promoted as the captain of Potiphar's guard. Black people and Joseph have been great inventors throughout slavery that gave them exceptional benefits over other slaves but the slave owners usually took credit for those inventions. After this newfound success, Potiphar's wife saw that Joseph was handsome and plotted a way for her to lie with him but against her wishes, Joseph would not sleep with her. Therefore, she told a lie on Joseph accusing him of rape causing Potiphar to have him thrown into prison. A host of black people generally speaking have been racially profiled and sent to prison for crimes they didn't commit. Many black men and women have even been brutally murdered based on what was verbally stated with no concrete evidence. Even if black people are justly found guilty, in 2018 black men alone made up over thirty-four percent of the prison population in the United States. This percentage is significantly higher than their brothers of other nationalities. This sets the stage for the last and final step for Joseph and the Black people. This last step is the Palace, for the first time in the history of the United States a black man was elected as President. Joseph represents that God is moving black people out of oppression and prison to the palace. Now that we know Joseph and the events that he went through in life are a direct correlation to the plight of black people in history. Joseph like black people have been hated by their brothers because of the coat of many gifts and talents their father God gave them to wear. We can sum this up by saying Joseph was hated by his brothers because of his skin color. Now on a Divine level, Joseph's coat that displayed the many gifts and talents of God's light given to men by its rainbow of colors also describes Jesus. Actually, it was three men who wore this same particular robe and had it stripped away from them by Satan, thinking that it would bring him Godly wisdom. These men were Adam, Joseph, and Jesus. Adam wore it as a fire of truth or wisdom that surrounded his body. Joseph wore it as a coat of many colors. Jesus wore it as a seamless robe that was rent from his body and raffled off at his crucifixion.

All three of these men were betrayed by the ones they loved. As stated before, we have to study the word of God in three realms: the realm of the father represented by Adam, the realm of this natural world which is the realm of the Flesh or the Son which is Joseph, the realm of the Holy Spirit which is Jesus who is the truth revealed to us by the Holy Spirit. This is the Holy Spirit revealing to us all the truths that we couldn't see when Jesus walked on earth as a fleshly man.

If you see Joseph as just being symbolic of Jesus; you are ignoring the other two realms of God. You are leaving out the fleshly aspects of Joseph that are symbolic to dark-skinned people destined for greatness. Black people were forced by their brothers into humility. All of this was done because of God's Divine plan for them to lead their brothers in the unfinished work of the cross. Let's look into some other symbolic aspects of Joseph's life. One of the most important things that were done to Joseph is that blood from an animal was used to cover up his gifts. We can sum the meaning of this with the word COVERT.

Covert: concealed; secret; disguised.

Animal sacrifice was used as atonement to cover up a man's sin before Jesus died and used his blood to cover every man's sin. How does this apply to Joseph or the Black man in the earthly realm? When his brothers dipped his coat of many gifts and talents in blood, their main objective was to cover up what they did to their brother. When you look at God and how He covers himself with the darkness of humility, we can see the Holy Ghost Revealing the covert operation of God. As mentioned before blood turns brown or black, so Joseph's coat was now as black as God's coat of humility. God said that He uses the secret of darkness as a part of his covert operation. God planned to keep Joseph's gifts a secret from the world until it was time for Joseph's gifts to make room for him. A secret that has yet to be revealed by God is a covenant. A covenant is like a sealed scroll that can only be opened at a specific time by the person or people it was meant for. The covenant like a contract contains the agreement of the people it was formed by. God uses this covenant as a seed that contains the legacies or the specific traits given by different trees that make up that covenant and seals them all as one within a seed. This is how one man by the name of Joseph can represent Adam, the black people, and his descendants that lead to Jesus. God always seals his covenant with blood symbolic of Joseph's brothers dipping his robe in the blood. Then God plants the seed of the covenant and grows it for its fruits to come to harvest at a specific time. Joseph was planted when he was thrown in the cistern by is his brothers. Next, God grew him into his purpose through very eventful stages along the way so that in the fullness of time he could fully represent the covenant his life was designed by God to fulfill. Well, how does this relate to the Black man? The Black man's history was covered up by God until the last days or the end of the age. He allowed his secret weapon not to be displayed until a world going to pieces could only be held together by the gifts of the sufferer, whom Joseph represents. God did this because His covert plan was not to just secretly get his Word back to the earth, but to keep a specific people's gift hidden even from themselves until it was time for them to lead through the power of humility and finish the work of carrying the Cross of Christ.

Joseph was the son of Jacob's old age. Jacob's old age represents the end of the era for the flesh symbolized by the end of Jesus' walk on earth as a carnal man. This was significant because the black man's gift would be called upon to carry Jesus' cross at this crucial point in Jesus' life. Joseph came along towards the end of his father Jacob's life symbolizing that black people's gifts wouldn't be called upon by God until the end times. This will be a time when all hope seems lost and people look upon God as if He really is not who He says He Is. This same disbelief was what the people felt as they looked at Jesus in pain as He struggled to carry the weight of the cross that signifies the weight of the world on His shoulders. Spectators observed Jesus as He was overcome by this weight as He walked and fell to the ground. As the difficult task of leadership during a time of famine would have overcome Pharaoh making room for Joseph to be the prince of Egypt; Jesus who was overcome by this same weight of responsibility made room for leadership by black people during these perilous times. . The people thought if He is truly Lord of ALL, He could carry that cross effortlessly all the way up the hill of Calvary. The world views the church today like people did Jesus at Calvary. No one is being healed, no signs, no wonders, no miracles. He saved others, let him save himself is their attitude. However, just when it seems like all hope is lost, God looks on a people that are represented by Joseph. Like Joseph, all these people had to help carry the weight of pain and suffrage was a dream. When all power seems to be drained from the church, God will place the burden of responsibility on the shoulders of a very gifted and talented people. These people were designed to carry the weight of suffrage effortlessly. Their stone is the Onyx stone; the stone that the builders rejected but now God has placed them as the keystone to bear the weight of responsibility. The Black man was designated and destined by God at the appointed time to handle the leadership responsibilities that come with carrying the cross the rest of the way until Jesus returns.

Dr. Martin Luther King Jr., who reflected the spiritual gifts of leadership and the talents of Joseph in this modern age, was also labeled a dreamer. His serious but peaceful nature reflected Joseph's gift to rise and flourish above anything. Dr. Martin Luther King Jr. played a key role in showing the world the plight of an oppressed people and revealing a future promise from God through a dream. Some say that Dr. Martin Luther King Jr. was a Moses to the black race, but his dream of the forgiveness of his brothers in the face of racism leans more toward Joseph. Joseph and Dr. Martin Luther King Jr. were both dreamers signifying their gift from God as visionaries to lead people through perilous times. These people, represented by Joseph, were brought low by their brothers while their cries and protest for help were ignored by their brothers. Their cries for mercy from the belly of ships were answered with the oppression of over four hundred years of slavery. These people had to look within their own hearts to find peace of mind when their loved one was subjected to all sorts of cruelty for no reason. This was a people that knew exactly what Jesus was going through, not because he did something wrong, but just because he was beloved and very gifted by His Father. These people suffered at the hands of their brothers just because their Father God covered them by planting them in the soils of humility growing them strong through history so that they would know how to lead from a standpoint of humility. Remember God rules from a standpoint of praise instead of pride, completion instead of competition, and compassion instead of arrogance. As stated before the Black men in America are in Prison. It's no coincidence that Joseph was in prison when Pharaoh sent for him. The centurion was looking for someone with a gift when he found Simon of Cyrene, just like the pharaoh was when he found Joseph. The Holy Spirit told me that Jesus and Simon of Cyrene were both represented by Joseph. Jesus represented the past age of the flesh that was about to be crucified and Simon represented a people that would be ushered in by the Holy Spirit. You can also look at it like this: Jesus as the Pharaoh or a King and Simon as Joseph who is the answer to King's Dream. In this same manner, Simon would also be the answer to Jesus's prayer in the Garden of Gethsemane when He asked His Father to take this cup from him as He sweated blood. God always steps in secretly. When it seems that weight is too much for us to bear He gives us someone who already knows your dream and they have been given the skill to easily work out things in your favor as an answer to your prayer. Why is this task that you must do so hard for yourself and so easy for them? God always sends you a person who not only knows what the problem is but also knows how to work the problem out. It was nothing for Joseph to interpret Pharaoh's dream and carry out the responsibilities of it, because Joseph had done those things on a daily basis for his father Israel, for Potiphar in slavery, and as a prison warden in prison.

It was nothing for Simon to carry the cross because it was a lifestyle for him already. Joseph was the one called on to help as Eve was created to be Adam's helper and as the Holy Spirit is our present help. Joseph, like Simon of Cyrene, had two sons representing that Joseph's and Simon's work wasn't finished but were a calling to responsibility, a call to duty, a call to order for black people who were once disorderly because they didn't know the truth.

Now, through this revelation, you have full knowledge of the truth. Realize that the calling, or the plight of the black man, is no different from what Jesus told his disciples when he said that the hardships that our ancestors endured had to take place.

The Apostles Paul said: Hebrews 12:1 KJV 1Wherefore seeing we also are compassed about with so great a cloud of witnesses, let us lay aside every weight, and the sin which doth so easily beset us, and let us run with patience the race that is set before us, 2Looking unto Jesus the author and finisher of our faith; who for the joy that was set before him endured the cross, despising the shame, and is set down at the right hand of the throne of God.

Can we take heed to this call to order as black people? Can we look at the joy that is set before us and lead with patience and humility as Jesus did? This call to order is the Revelation Knowledge of The Truth that is being given to Black people, who are in the pig pin of their existence so that they may come to themselves and turn back to their Heavenly Father just like the prodigal son returned to his father. God looks upon the Black people as a prodigy who is a person, endowed with exceptional qualities or abilities like Joseph. However, they are living prodigally which means they are wasting their talents and abilities in the world instead of using them in God's vineyards. Now that we have come to ourselves, we know that we are the beloved of our Father God and He is looking and waiting on us. He will forgive our sins before we even ask Him because He is filled with compassion for us. He will run to us, put his arms around us, and welcome us with a kiss.

Father God will give you back your true identity by telling His servants to quickly bring the best Robe and put it on your shoulders. God will take the shame of slavery away by putting shoes on our feet. He will restore your inheritance by placing the ring of sonship on your finger. Even though your brothers will be angry, the Father God himself will plead your court case with him to make him see the light on your behalf.

Luke 15:22-31 NIV

But the father said to his servants, 'Quick! Bring the best robe and put it on him. Put a ring on his finger and sandals on his feet. 23 Bring the fattened calf and kill it. Let's have a feast and celebrate. 24 For this son of mine was dead and is alive again; he was lost and is found.' So they began to celebrate.

25 "Meanwhile, the older son was in the field. When he came near the house, he heard music and dancing. 26 So he called one of the servants and asked him what was going on. 27 'Your brother has come,' he replied, 'and your father has killed the fattened calf because he has him back safe and sound.'

28 "The older brother became angry and refused to go in. So his father went out and pleaded with him. 29 But he answered his father, 'Look! All these years I've been slaving for you and never disobeyed your orders. Yet you never gave me even a young goat so I could celebrate with my friends. 30 But when this son of yours who has squandered your property with prostitutes comes home, you kill the fattened calf for him!'

31 "'My son,' the father said, 'you are always with me, and everything I have is yours. 32 But we had to celebrate and be glad, because this brother of yours was dead and is alive again; he was lost and is found.'"

TRANSFIGURATION AND TRANSPARENCY

The Mountain of Transfiguration, or the Mountain of Transparency, is where Jesus was transfigured before the eyes of His Disciples. Jesus's transfiguration represented the pureness of Jesus's Spirit, Soul, and Body and was indicative of the fact that all three of these beings were fused as one without any confusion of sin. These three beings that make up our savior Jesus Christ are known as The Father, Son, and Holy Spirit. They are joined with no corruption. Christ's three-part being are in perfect alignment with the Mind of GOD, meaning that they are all one, being governed by one mind. Unlike Jesus, His Disciples are of two minds: a spiritual mind that is of God and a fleshly mind that is of Satan. These two minds have their roots in the double-minded Tree of The KNOWLEDGE of Good and Evil in the Garden of Eden which keeps our spirit, soul, and body at war with themselves.

We, like the Disciples, have a disagreement going on with our three-part being that will not allow us to be transfigured because the FIRE OF

TRUTH would destroy us instead of changing us simply because our three-part being is not in total alliance with God's Truth.

Jesus however came into contact with the heat produced by the FIRE of TRUTH, which is the Holy Spirit. A miraculous molecular change started to take place in His fleshly body right before the eyes of His Disciples. Let's see exactly how the Bible describes this miraculous event. As you read notice how the Word of God specifically points out that after six days had passed and keep in mind that 7 is the number of The Fire of Truth or The Holy Spirit.

Matthew 17: 2-8 New International Versions (NIV)

The Transfiguration
17 After six days Jesus took with him Peter, James and John the brother of James, and led them up a high mountain by themselves. 2 There he was transfigured before them. His face shone like the sun, and his clothes became as white as the light. 3 Just then there appeared before them Moses and Elijah, talking with Jesus.

4 Peter said to Jesus, "Lord, it is good for us to be here. If you wish, I will put up three shelters—one for you, one for Moses and one for Elijah."

5 While he was still speaking, a bright cloud covered them, and a voice from the cloud said, "This is my Son, whom I love; with him I am well pleased. Listen to him!" 6 When the disciples heard this, they fell facedown to the ground, terrified. 7 But Jesus came and touched them. "Get up," he said. "Don't be afraid." 8 When they looked up, they saw no one except Jesus.

Let's focus on Jesus' face and clothes. The Word says his face shone like the sun and his clothes became white as light. Jesus entered the spiritual realm and the very FIRE OF THE HOLY SPIRIT affected Jesus's flesh the way God purposely designed it from the beginning when he created man from the dust of the earth. This is a reason why God created man from the dust, or sand which was for our bodies to Glorify God. When the Apostle Paul speaks of Adam's earthly body he is speaking of his earthly body after sin. Apostle Paul mentioned that Adam's sin-corrupted body was perishable because, before sin, Adam's body was not perishable.

Jesus' body Glows or is glorified. So is his clothing which is also shining and the fire is not burning Jesus's clothing. Why is this?

1ˢᵗ Corinthians 15:46-53 TLB
46 First, then, we have these human bodies, and later on God gives us spiritual, heavenly bodies. 47 Adam was made from the dust of the earth, but Christ came from heaven above. 48 Every human being has a body just like Adam's, made of dust, but all who become Christ's will have the same kind of body as his—a body from heaven. 49 Just as each of us now has a body like Adam's, so we shall someday have a body like Christ's.

50 I tell you this, my brothers: an earthly body made of flesh and blood cannot get into God's Kingdom. These perishable bodies of ours are not the right kind to live forever.

51 But I am telling you this strange and wonderful secret: we shall not all die, but we shall all be given new bodies! 52 It will all happen in a moment, in the twinkling of an eye, when the last trumpet is blown. For there will be a trumpet blast from the sky,[f] and all the Christians who have died will suddenly become alive, with new bodies that will never, never die; and then we who are still alive shall suddenly have new bodies too. 53 For our earthly bodies, the ones we have now that can die, must be transformed into heavenly bodies that cannot perish but will live forever.

This is how the Holy Spirit explained the process of Transfiguration that will happen in a split second. The process of turning sand into glass requires heat just like any refined substance. We have to refine things with fire to obtain a pure, unadulterated form. Sand liquefies and glows with a bright luminance and takes on a transparent form called glass. Other forms of purification called recrystallization are used in the refineries of most glass manufacturers.

Now the Holy Spirit did not tell me that our Glorified Heavenly Bodies would be made from glass. The substance that our flesh would be changed into was not revealed. The Holy Spirit did say that the purification of the flesh would be like a refinery produces glass from sand. He also revealed that the heat from the Fire of Truth that burns within our hearts will keep our love from waxing cold and keep us at the right temperature to be transparent and malleable. Our malleable bodies will allow us to move and flex. Just like our fleshly bodies are now at the right temperature outside, as you go inward toward the heart our temperature rises. Without the warm blood pumping from our hearts, our bodies would harden into a rigor mortis state. To wax, cold was a term used by Jesus to show that love can grow cold in the spirit like your blood grows cold in the natural. The hardening of either of them in both realms results in rigor-mortis. However, after we are transfigured we will never die because the Spirit of Truth will always be burning within us.

The transparency of Man's flesh shows that he has been purified by the fire of the Holy Spirit that rids him of all corruption that would come into conflict with the Fire of Truth. Remember the Fire of Truth only consumes sin or corruption. The Word of God says that man will put off corruption and put on incorruption; meaning that our corrupt bodies must be changed into incorruptible bodies so we won't be consumed by God's Fire of Truth. The sinful part of us that cannot stand the intense heat of God's presence will instantly be consumed by the fire of The Holy Spirit. After the sin is consumed by the heat, the remnants of Man's flesh will be free of all the impurities of sin, shining like the sun and magnifying the magnificent Light or knowledge of God's Truth. The glorified body of man along with his spirit and soul will be purified with the Fire of The Holy Spirit forming one being. He will shine with the pure light of truth like Jesus did on the Mountain of Transfiguration. This will fulfill the covenant that God made to Noah that he will not cleanse the earth with water, but with the Fire of Purification.

COMPLETION REPLACES COMPETITION

What God has revealed through the Revelation of the Rainbow and the Tower of Babel is that his Church will go through a process of purification like Esther did in the Old Testament. The result will be a church without spot or blemish, perfect in all of its ways, just like her husband our Lord and Savior Jesus Christ. Until then, she will learn patience and forbearance; she will have to learn how to look from the inside out like her husband to be.

The church, like the world, is now looking from the outside in. As we discussed in the chapter entitled The Rainbow of Spiritual Gifts, God's perspective is from the inside out which represents humility. However, there is another perspective that is looking from the outside in. This way of perceiving the world is Satan's perspective, which is also his system of pride. This system judges what is on the outside without paying any attention to what lies just beneath the surface. This is how Satan tricked Eve. The Word of God says Eve saw that the fruit was pleasing to the eye. Then she ate, taking for granted what she had already heard about the fruit from Adam. Satan desires to break into what God has already established and take over. This process is totally different from God's approach of humility, which is to begin as a child like a seed and grow into whatever it is that you need. Satan does not look out from where he is to grow or achieve it rightfully, but rather to break into whatever he wants and possess it. Satan's standpoint is called self-centeredness. This point of view takes for granted what someone else desires by forcing their own aspirations over others, even if it means eliminating them in the process. This is called competition. Competition is where one must eliminate his opponent to get what he has or to achieve something that both opponents want. This perspective of self-centeredness was seen with Satan exalting his will to rule over earth and man, to the point that he used trickery ultimately paving the way to the death of mankind. Then, after Satan became the governing force by putting man into the bondage of slavery, he passed that competitive viewpoint down through Adam to his sons Cain and Abel. Cain killing his brother Abel was the first example of elimination under the system of competition. From this point on throughout history, man has killed to be at the top. He has created competitive sports to satisfy his desire to determine who is the best. For this reason, we train "athletes" and form them into superb, almost flawless beings, of whatever their competitive craft is. We even have formed militias to protect ourselves from our own brothers because of this competitive, deceitful, sinful nature that we all inherited from Satan. This competitive nature has even infiltrated itself into the church of God where people compete for leadership and downplay unseen roles that don't require a front center position.

Competition has church leaders playing their members' gifts against other members to see who does the best at operating within the church. This result has split churches that consist of backstabbing members, using deceitful measures to make the next member look bad in the leader's eyes. This type of competition can be found throughout the Body of Christ.

This trail of blood caused by our competitive nature will increase more and more leading up to the battle of Armageddon. If we look closely, we can see that it's all because of Lucifer who desired God's throne. In Heaven, Lucifer tried to use this method of competition to eliminate God. Lucifer desired to break through the front lines of Heaven to get to the treasure in the middle of the rainbow, which is the throne of God.

Man's most popular sports are the ones that use this same technique. One has to break through the lines of defense representing the different bands of color in the rainbow to achieve a touchdown or to slam dunk or even get to home plate. What man is trying to protect is what he reveres and what man reveres is his treasure. This center spot; is where man's heart is. In sports, this place is called the goal. This area represents what would be the throne of God. The enemy tries to take this throne by using deceit. In the world of sports, we call these different levels of trickery or plays. In war, we call them tactics. The Word of God calls them devices. This is how Satan plays siblings against siblings, family members against family members, people against people, churches against churches, and nations against nations.

Man has fallen away from God's method to the point that he considers God's perspective of humility to be foreign and Satan's point of view of competition as domestic. No one person can have this treasure because everybody wants it for themselves. In sports, we call this treasure a trophy. This award method is Satan's way of keeping man competing for the same thing over and over to achieve what he wants but we can never truly possess it. This repetitious form of slavery is like man building the Tower of Babel, layer by layer, driven by pride with a false sense of hope that he would reach Heaven. However; God knows mankind will always come short of reaching this goal without the atonement of His son Jesus. One may ask why this is? The answer is because every man has sinned and fallen short of the Glory. In other words, God says that mankind train and fight every day of their lives while only obtaining a small piece of what they think is Heaven. Then after they get a little slice of their own version of Heaven, they realize it falls short of providing perfect peace and eternal life. Mankind must strive continuously because the satisfaction of obtaining their treasure is temporal. Then the demanding race of striving to get more to add to what they have is coupled with the fear of someone taking the little they've obtained.

Men on their own will never be able to achieve the full Glory that only can be realized through the Lord Jesus Christ. Jesus brings the Light of Truth which is the mind of the father back to men. Adam separated himself and the human race from God's Light of Truth when he ate the forbidden fruit in the garden. Before Adam rebelled, the Light of Truth that is commonly referred to as Glory illuminated his body like it did the body of Jesus on the Mountain of Transfiguration. . This Glory was physical evidence that Adam had the wisdom, knowledge, and understanding of his Father that empowered him not only to get wealth but to live with it in peace eternally. In the Garden of Eden, Satan deceived man out of his wealth by stripping him of his robe of Glory leaving him naked and in the chains of slavery. Satan stole man's birthright as Jacob did to his brother Esau. Now he holds that same promise of riches and Glory over man's head to keep him striving for something he can never attain without Jesus. Satan now offers this robe of glory to man, in exchange for his soul.

Satan wants more than an arm and a leg; he wants what he didn't pay for and that is man's soul. The only way one can pay full price for the life of another is to give up one's own. Jesus is the only man that loved his brother to the point of giving up his life for him. This system of competition is empowered by slavery. The corporate world uses this technique to bind workers as slaves and locks them into a competitive cycle fueled by their own greed. This aggressive race is an endless cycle of greed commonly known as keeping up with the Jones' which fuels this system of debt. This system is lorded over by Satan himself. With his system of usury, Satan keeps us constantly paying a debt that we can never pay off on our own. Satan has the world, and most of the church, locked into his method of using money that's not theirs to get what they want. However; there is another system that was taken from the minds of men that is based on the principle of humility. This method entered back into the kingdom of this world as a child. Even though He was the Son of The King he was born in a stable thus exercising the perfect principle of humility. Baby Jesus the second Adam and the future Savior of mankind lay among animals much like the previous Adam. These were humble beginnings, to say the least. However, His Father in Heaven purposely planted Him in the heart of humility so His system could grow throughout the earth

With His Knowledge of Truth, Jesus set the slaves free from their bondage to Satan. God's system of giving His Seed shows man that you have to be established from within and grow outward as opposed to Satan who takes and forces his way in. This system of Peace that comes from giving is the system God put in effect in Eden. The Garden of Eden represents the place that lies in the center of our hearts.

God started humans and animals with just one male and female, and not 200 of each kind because the system of giving through humility allows things to grow through multiplication. This system allowed God to establish his covenant with the first man so that His legacy of perfect order could be inherited and passed down for generations. This is the system of God from a standpoint of humility looking outward to help others and not looking inward which is known as self-centeredness. The process of giving your own gift instead of trying to take someone else's gift is called completion. Completion comes from the word complete.

This brings us right back to the rainbow displaying the different gifts of the different groups of people placed in perfect order according to how it pleases God. From Adam and Eve, throughout the generations, God has given mankind different gifts that He has placed in a specific order These gifts were never meant to compete with another's gift like in a game of war but to complete the other like the organs in our bodies. What would the heart be if it was in competition with the blood? This would cause both to waste away because one can't function without the other. To understand this process of completion, let's look at the earth as a man using the oceans as his body and the different landmasses as the resources that the organs would use to sustain this mighty living body called earth. Now, the different groups of people that were dispersed throughout the earth from Babel are the living organs that turn the different resources into vital substances needed to sustain the mighty life of Earth. Now if all the different continents of people work together and give of their gifts and talents then everyone would have all sufficiency in all things. This means every group on every continent that represents a functioning organ would have exactly what it needs not to want for anything. As men, we use the tools or gifts that God gives us to sustain ourselves and others. Therefore like God; this being that is named earth now thrives from the inside out. We used this as an analogy, but this shows exactly how God intended the earth to be ruled when he created Eden. Adam and Eve would be the center of command, ruling through love because Adam would have the same mind as Christ and the government would be on his shoulders. Eden would be the heart and mind of the earth. All of us who are his children would spread out over the different continents giving of our gifts from the first fruits of our land to our brothers until all nations of the earth are blessed. This is how the gifts are really supposed to work.

Our gifts then start to make room for us in our brothers' hearts. There is a void within your brother's heart for your gift or your people's gift. This could be an office space in your brother's company or a position in his kingdom. Joseph is a perfect example of how his gift made room for him in Potiphar's house, in prison, and the palace. The prophet Daniel is another example of how his gift made room for him with King Nebuchadnezzar. The Garden of Eden's system of giving allows one brother to gladly edify the other by fulfilling his needs. The Word of God directly supports Eden's System of Completion where one would gain by cheerfully giving of oneself.

Luke 6:38 KJV
38Give, and it shall be given unto you; good measure, pressed down, and shaken together, and running over, shall MEN give into your bosom. For with the same measure that ye mete withal it shall be measured to you again.

Jesus explained the perfect system of Eden in perfect detail to his disciples and the people in the Sermon on the Mount long after the Kingdom of Eden passed. Man's cheerful giving gave way to selfish living as Satan forced his system of competition on man. Man, now feared that his brother's gift would be favored by God more than his. As a result of this fear, men began to kill their brothers in a never-ending, cycle of strife. Greed fueled by fear now caused man to covet his brother's gift. Unwilling to freely give of his gift he now selfishly takes his brother's gift making himself rich by oppressing his brother. Man wants to control God's entire rainbow of gifts to men and use them by force for his own personal gain as with Jacob and Esau.

Jacob wanted his father's blessing that was meant for the first born son Esau. He resorted to trickery to take his brother's blessing; a clever scheme that was orchestrated against his Father Isaac by their mother Rebecca. This plight to deceive Abraham's son Isaac shows just how important to success a blessing can be that is passed down within a particular family group or nation. For this reason, a person's gift can be coveted by another family member. For this same reason, Joseph was hated by his brothers.

Let Joseph's brothers represent the different races of people in the world. Even though they were his brothers and they originated from the same father, they still hated Joseph because of his gift. Remember the Gift of a particular family group is characterized by the pigment of their skin. Joseph was very gifted, represented by the rainbow-colored coat that his father made for him. Joseph's coat of many colors coupled with his dream caused his brothers to hate him. Joseph's brothers competitive nature wouldn't allow them to see his gift as a blessing; instead, they viewed it as a threat. As a result, they began to think of ways to segregate themselves from Joseph. Joseph thrived even though his brothers conspired against him by stripping him of his identity and selling him into slavery. Every situation that Joseph was placed into his gifts were used as a tool making him a ruler over it. The coat of many colors symbolically represents the many different shades of human skin pigments. These different colors refer to a rainbow of gifts that God gave to man.

What we call racism is actually a nationality or a family group of people that hates another nationality because of their distinct differences, such as, skin color, which represents their God-given gift. We can also take it a step further and see that Joseph's coat of many different colors meant that the more colors you have, the more gifted you are and the more you are hated. Darkness or the color black has all the different colors of the spectrum within it just like Joseph's coat. This means the brothers that are wearing this darker skin color are very gifted and are the most hated of all the brothers.

His brothers desired to strip Joseph of his identity by taking off his coat and dipping it in blood. They didn't know that what they saw on the outside of Joseph was just a representation of the leadership qualities that God had placed within Joseph and it could not be stripped away. The next time they saw Joseph he was the prince of Egypt.

As a result of Joseph being in the place God desired for him to be, all of his brothers representing all races or nations of the earth were blessed. Completion makes us complete because our gift gives us the grace to fulfill the need in our brothers' lives with ease. In this way, we complement each other through humility or praise as in a marriage submitting ourselves to one another as a husband and wife. Just as the two are joined together to become one body, in that same way the races of the brothers and sisters of the body of believers must complement the other by giving of themselves gladly to the other. In return, they all receive abundance and enjoy great satisfaction. These gifts then multiply into more blessings that you would desire, just as sex makes a multiplicity of children that are a blessing for a married couple.

With completion, each of the seven nations of the earth realized that they belong to a body that thrives because each organ does something different as they put their many different gifts to work. The product that is produced by those seven different gifts is what we call the fruits of the spirit. There are twelve fruits of the Holy Spirit produced from those seven gifts.

As believers, we are the body of Christ which is also known as the Bride of Christ. However, before we can be married to our husband Jesus, we must first join each other in total submission unto one another in love as Christ loves us or the church. So, the principle of what is manifested on the outside must first take place on the inside. In other words, before we can become joined with Christ outwardly as His bride, we must be joined together genuinely within as brothers into one Church.

We must first see praise not just as a song of reverence, but as a language. Praise is the language of humility and only the humble can understand it.

Psalm 34: 1-3 King James Version (KJV)
1 I will bless the Lord at all times: his praise shall continually be in my mouth.
2 My soul shall make her boast in the Lord: the humble shall hear thereof, and be glad.
3 O magnify the Lord with me, and let us exalt his name together.

In Verse 2, when we do not have the spirit of competition, we make our boast in the Lord instead of boasting in ourselves. Making our boast in the Lord is true praise. Those that operate in the Spirit of humility will be able to understand why we are making our boast in the Lord. They understand the language of humility which is praise. Praise is a language based on the principle that it's better to give than to receive. When our family communicates this language of praise, they are glad. Remember that God loves a cheerful giver. After everyone begins to operate in a spirit of praise, they build a synergistic tower of praise by exalting the Lord together in Word and deed. Praise is the international language of the seven nations. This language will unite them like they were at Babel. Instead of Nimrod, Jesus will be their leader. The tower of the Lord Jesus is called the Name of The Lord. Only the righteous can comprehend the language of humility to enter into this mighty tower of safety.

Isaiah 2 New International Version (NIV)

The Mountain of the Lord
2 This is what Isaiah son of Amos saw concerning Judah
and Jerusalem:
In the last days
The mountain of the Lord's temple will be established
As the highest of the mountains;
it will be exalted above the hills,
and all nations will stream to it.

This Tower of Praise that Isaiah is speaking of is constructed like the Tower of Babel. The Tower of Praise is built by the synergetic power of the minds of the believers casting down their own fleshly agenda so that they may see the Light of God. God's plan of reconciliation was to get His Marvelous Light back into the minds of men so that they may receive instruction on how to build this temple. However, before this temple can be established in the natural, it first must be established in the Spirit. As the people of Babel exalted a tower of their own will against God we exalt our own will and opinions before God's knowledge. By casting down our will, God's Spiritual Tower of Truth can be built. We humble ourselves so Jesus can be lifted. Jesus said, "if I am lifted from the Earth I will draw all men unto me." Also, this word is confirmed in Micah 4 NIV

Micah 4 New International Version (NIV)
The Mountain of the Lord
4 In the last days
the mountain of the Lord's temple will be established
as the highest of the mountains;
it will be exalted above the hills,
and peoples will stream to it.

The temple on the mount is the Tower of Truth spoken about in Proverbs 18:10 in the (NIV):

10 The name of the Lord is a fortified tower;
the righteous run to it and are safe.

The Tower of Truth is the Tower of Light. All the gifts given to man by the Holy Spirit of Truth represent all of the nations within it, operating collectively according to how God placed them. What does this tower paint a perfect picture of? The answer is the rainbow.

The Rainbow is exalted as a promise that man ultimately has a Tower of Truth to run to and be saved like Noah was saved from the flood. Jesus told Peter that on this mountain of Revelation I will build my Tower of Truth and the gates of hell will not prevail against it. This starts with viewing God as the center of everything that we do. In The city of Truth where the mountain of Truth is located its citizens can only speak the international language of humility. This is the language of praise. To communicate and live with our brothers, this language must be spoken continually. When we truly learn to speak this language and live it, God's purpose will be manifested on earth. The language of praise is not just a language by itself. This Heavenly language of praise also has a culture that goes along with it.

Just like in England, you have the English language, but you also have the English Culture to go along with that language. Even if no word is spoken one can observe their everyday activities and predict the language they speak. If you are in England, you should be prepared to drink tea at least once a day if you want to fit in with the culture. The same goes for the Kingdom of Heaven and the Tower of Praise. There are certain qualities that one possesses not as a religious activity, but as a normal way of life. As the world sees these various distinctions, they will know that we are believers. These different qualities fall into one category called love. People will know us through our love. This love is birthed out of a culture of humility. There are also powerful supernatural manifestations that follow believers that reside in that city. These powerful manifestations are called signs.

THE CULTURE BEHIND THE LANGUAGE

As we take a closer look into this culture we begin to understand the lifestyle of Adam and Eve in the Garden of Eden. One may ask why we always end up in the Garden of Eden. The Garden of Eden is a perfect reference point because it represents God's perfect will for mankind. Eden's culture can be defined as a utopia that stemmed from its pleasure in giving. Everything about the Garden Life was joyous giving. As stated earlier, Adam had a connection with the earth like he had with his wife Eve.

Isaiah55:12-13 KJV
For ye shall go out with joy, and be led forth with peace: the mountains and the hills shall break forth before you into singing, and all the trees of the field shall clap their hands.

The earth was glad to give of itself to Adam and there was no pain inflicted on the earth because Adam didn't till the soil. The earth had freely opened itself for Adam's Seed. It was truly a joy for the earth to give of itself according to what it was created to do by God for Adam. Ephesians 5:21 is one of the main principles of this culture.

Eph5:21KJV
Submitting yourselves one to another in the fear of God.

Under this principle, everything was completed and this perfect system that God put in place was good. Eve and the Earth gave back to the center of who they were connected to and that person was Adam. Adam was created from the Earth and Eve was created from Adam. Earth, Adam, and Eve were connected like the Father, Son, and the Holy Spirit. This means everything of the Earth, from the atmosphere to the water, to the land, and the Earth's fiery core, obeyed Adam gladly. Not only did the Earth give itself gladly to Adam but the creatures loved and reverenced Adam too. Adam was their direct connection to God. God made this connection possible through Adam's flesh because they were made from the same substance. This means that the Earth, Adam, and Eve all formed one body. Eve and Adam shared the same connectivity as the Earth did with Adam. In many ways the Earth and Eve parallel, which is all a part of God's perfect order.

One of the most obvious parallels of the Earth and Eve is their complex makeup giving them the ability to reproduce life. Earth and Eve are alike in such a way that if their similarities are understood correctly it will help couples to have more peace in their marriage. Couples would be able to accurately identify and shun those sin traits that are passed from Satan and quickly brushed off as instinctive behavior.

Eve and her daughters were designed by God to be just like Earth down to the last detail. Now, we wouldn't say that they look the same because Eve was a woman made in the image of God. Being made in the image of Heaven, Earth was ruled by Adam as Heaven is by God. A woman can directly relate to the Earth as it pertains to the pain caused by the metal plow of man. The ground is literally pierced and turned inside out to make it conducive for the seed. A woman can explain exactly how the Earth feels during the cultivation process because this same pain can be felt by her in childbirth. Keep in mind: these are after sin traits for the Earth and the woman. Before sin, there wasn't any pain for Earth or Women; it would have been the opposite. Yes, it would have been a joy in childbirth and the Earth would gladly open up for the seed because there was only joy associated with giving of oneself for the benefit of another. The Word says the blessing of God makes you rich and he adds no sorrow to it. No one had any knowledge of sorrow until the fall of man. Now, because of sin, we experience the pain that is a consequence of our sin.

For example, for every birth, there is going to be a death. This excruciating pain that we all experience is called sacrifice. We didn't know pain until we gained this knowledge by eating from the Tree of Knowledge of Good and Evil that added an evil thing to every good thing that happens to us. That word AND is used as a conjunction to add evil to Good; the same way it's used to join man and woman together in marriage. In this union, they became one. You can't have one without the other. Before man ate of the tree, he did not know evil. Now because of this additional evil DNA trait that was added to man, evil follows man's good throughout his life on Earth.

The Apostle Paul said it best, "when I try to do good, evil is right there with me." We now know through Revelation knowledge that these issues of man are not merely instinctive and natural, but are evil traits that don't reflect the perfect Earth and Man that both were declared good by God after He created them. Now that we have determined the Good and Evil traits inherited by Women and the Earth, we can compare the Earth's ever-changing unpredictable weather and natural disasters to her ever-changing mood swings. Before sin, the Earth's weather was consistently perfect like God who designed it. You can see this consistency in the weather all the way up to Noah when the Word of God states that it had never rained on Earth. This also represents Eve's attitude that was the same every day. Her sin-cursed body is as moody as the Earth's weather. A woman can relate to how hard it is for her husband to cope with her mood swings. She only has to feel the heat or the cold; the severity of storms or the sudden earthquakes that Earth throws upon her and her family. Even though we have meteorologists and seismologists to help us try to predict these changing events, neither woman nor man can know what to expect from the Earth.

God never intended for humankind to be unpredictable. Women, God didn't wire you like that; sin did. God is just and never changing; we as men and women were created to be that way also. To be unjust is to be double-minded knowing both good and evil. *As it says in James 1:6-7 NIV: the one who doubts is like a wave of the sea, blown and tossed away by the wind.* The Word of God is comparing a doubtful, sin-infected man to the ever-changing weather of this sin-cursed earth. This person should not expect to receive anything from the Lord because such a person is double-minded and unstable.

The last parallel of Eve and Earth carries with it the desire for independence and dominance. This last parallel will be hard to fathom for so many Christian women and men, who live in this age of independence and equality. Disclaimer: I believe that women should have the same rights as men and I'm not chauvinistic; however we must remember that God's principle of humility always sees the other person's needs above their own. This will be more readily accepted when I explain the role of man and how it parallels God.

To the woman, God said your desire shall be for your husband. Here desire means to lust for power, not sexual lust. Women will desire to rule over and dominate their husbands like Satan desires the very throne of God. The word desire doesn't mean that woman desires to co-rule with her husband in power but to remove her husband from his throne by elimination. Remember Satan's way is to eliminate his opponent through competition.

Now because of sin, the woman that once took Adam's concerns to heart has become a stranger to Adam preferring her new ways. The Bible speaks of Eve's ways toward Adam in Proverbs. 5 as if this chapter was actually the conversation that God was telling Adam not to follow in Eve's path.

Proverbs5:2-6 KJV
2 That thou mayest regard discretion, and that thy lips may keep knowledge.
3 For the lips of a strange woman drop as an honeycomb, and her mouth is smoother than oil:
4 But her end is bitter as wormwood, sharp as a two-edged sword.
5 Her feet go down to death; her steps take hold on hell.
6 Lest thou shouldest ponder the path of life, her ways are moveable, that thou canst not know them.

This whole chapter is about God describing to Adam what his fate will be if he follows in his wife's path in her fallen state. However, God describes her ways as so moveable, that Adam wouldn't be able to understand her. What a piece of work Adam's wife has become by plotting with Satan to kill her husband. In Genesis, you will see that after Satan had guided Eve's lips to deceive Adam to sin, something else became cursed in the process of Adam's rebellion. Now, this thing was out to get both Adam and his Wife. If you are thinking that it was the Serpent, you are partially right. Adam's biggest threat to him and his wife was the Earth He lived on. God said because of you, Adam, cursed is the ground. The Earth used to open itself up for Adam and shout for Joy, now the Earth wanted to rid itself of him. Adam being cautious of his wife now had to shelter himself from the Earth as well.

Now it can be seen why man must adapt to Earth's ever-changing environment rather than having a peaceful existence through consistent stability. We all know the dangers of unstable weather representing the inconsistencies of man. Jesus' disciples experienced this inconsistency in weather as Jesus lay sleeping on their sea-tossed vessel. Jesus didn't experience the storm that was so threatening to His disciples because He had a steadfast mindset and a peaceful mood throughout the storm. His disciples were constantly being tossed back and forth becoming victims of their ignorant, unstable, natural minds.

Jesus' behavior was conducive to the Garden of Eden's environment because His peaceful environment on the inside superseded the natural environment on the outside. This environment of Heaven can only be achieved by a consistent mindset that is not moved by different moods caused by the issues of this World. The Word of God calls this type of mindset a sound mind. Now because Jesus had the calm mind of His Father He was in Perfect Peace. Jesus could now easily manifest this peace that was on the inside of him by speaking it into existence because his heart was filled with this peace. So when Jesus spoke, that which was inside his heart, immediately manifested into the natural world. The abundance of Perfect Peace in the heart of Jesus became a way of life for Him externally.

Therefore your flesh can only manifest on the outside what you have in abundance on the inside. The more Revelation knowledge you have of God's Word, the more Peace you can manifest in the Earth. Peace is a byproduct of the sound, consistent mind of God. The disciples lack of inner awareness caused them to be moved by the storm unlike Jesus's firm understanding of the Word that made Him steadfast.

Jesus questioned his disciples about their faith; because faith is knowing that what you can't see is reality and rules over what you can see. God's will is for man to live and not die and proclaim the wonderful works of God. When you put your trust in God's will, the foundation is laid which is the stability of your faith. Knowing the unchanging will of God for one's life births faith because the Word of God says that Faith begins where the will of God is known. The will of God is for us to know His mind.

We can only know the mind of God by carefully studying the written Word. Then as we listen to a minister relay revelation knowledge of this written word one's faith is grown. The Holy Spirit sheds light on what they have read which establishes understanding. This spoken Word is imperative for young Christians who haven't learned to hear the Holy Spirit and for mature Christians that need spiritual guidance essential to growth. How can we hear the Word of God without a Preacher? It doesn't matter how much Revelation knowledge you have it is important that you submit to spiritual authority and guidance.

God told Adam because your flesh is cursed that which your flesh originated from is cursed also. Just like the Tree of the Knowledge of Good and Evil added Evil to man's flesh, it caused Earth to have Evil added to it as well. Since Earth is the Mother of all-natural creation everything that came from her became unstable. Animals begin to act abnormally and instead of living at peace with each other, they began to devour one another. As a result, each animal had to protect itself from the other. Everything born to the mother of all mankind received this bipolar, unstable curse of confusion. Disconnected from the sound mind of God mankind is subject to emotional instability and indecisiveness that are also connected to the curse. We can't make up our minds because we have been deprived of Devine intelligence. God said that His people suffer because they don't have His sound stable mind which is a rock that can't be moved. Jesus is that rock symbolizing the sound mind of God that was sent to be planted as a seed of wisdom in the minds of men so we can know Him.

When we accept Jesus into our hearts we are actually accepting God's sound mind to rule over our lives. Now that we have the sound mind of God, we have something to lean on when faced with adversity as a house is supported by a firm foundation. Proverbs 3:5-6 (TLB), Lean not to your own understanding, but it in all your WAYS acknowledge Him and He will direct your path. Notice the word "ways" in Proverbs

3:6. (TLB). What about the word *ways* that the Holy Spirit continues to emphasize? Remember Eve's ways were movable so that Adam could not understand them. God wants mankind to consider their ways. The Latin definition for the word Ways:

> *Origin for modus operandi: from Latin. Word Origin and History for modus operandi. "way of doing or accomplishing,"*

The word way means your mode for accomplishing something. Accomplishing what? If you look at the Latin meaning for the word accomplish, it means to fill up or to fulfill. God is telling us that our ways are the modes of operation that He gave us to manifest our desires, whether we want them to be manifested or not. The word manifest means to display or show (a quality or feeling) by one's acts or appearance; to demonstrate.

So, if we step back to where Jesus was asleep on the boat we can see that Jesus was manifesting signs of peace by his actions before the disciples awakened Him. Jesus' sleeping displayed evidence of the perfect peace that was abundant on the inside of his heart. When Jesus spoke, the abundance of Perfect Peace in His heart coupled with his peaceful ways the issue of his heart began to **flow out** and **fill up** his physical surroundings. When we live purpose-driven lives of humility, this produces a climate of peace. This is the climate that is necessary to grow the seed that came from the midst of the fruit of wisdom that God planted in the center of the Garden of Eden. The Tree of Life can only grow and flourish in these favorable conditions. This is the reason Jesus was able to sleep during the Storm on the Sea.

Proverbs 3:16-26 TLB
16-17 Wisdom gives: a long, good life, riches, honor, pleasure, peace. 18 Wisdom is a tree of life to those who eat her fruit; happy is the man who keeps on eating it.

> *19 The Lord's wisdom founded the earth; his understanding established all the universe and space. 20 The deep fountains of the earth were broken open by his knowledge, and the skies poured down rain.*
>
> *21 Have two goals: wisdom—that is, knowing and doing right—and common sense. Don't let them slip away, 22 for they fill you with living energy and bring you honor and respect.[b] 23 They keep you safe from defeat and disaster and from stumbling off the trail. 24-26 With them on guard you can sleep without fear; you need not be afraid of disaster or the plots of wicked men, for the Lord is with you; he protects you.*

Our ways are powerful vessels given to us by God. He has given us these vessels to be filled by our words and manifest His will on earth. In our ignorance, this tool has been taken for granted endangering ourselves and others by manifesting the genuine evil intentions of our hearts. Our ways manifest the intentional motives of our hearts even though we may try to disguise them. We have all heard the phrase before: ***Isn't it funny how the way you feel shows on your face?*** Your flesh was designed by God to manifest your spirit into this natural realm. So, your smile or frown isn't just a facial expression, it's also a spiritual manifestation. The condition of our heart affects the way we feel and the way we feel affects our ways. Our ways in return manifest the way we feel in our hearts to the physical world. The earth manifested the cursed state of its unstable core through storms, volcanoes, earthquakes, and landslides. Earth's instability, makes it a danger to itself and its inhabitants. In this manner we also have an atmosphere surrounding us, radiating either good or bad from energy from the core of our beings which are our hearts. We call these vibes. Vibes from a person's heart are radiated as emotions resulting in either good or bad reactions. The Energy that surrounds the Earth is called weather. The Energy that surrounds humans is also called weather that originates from our core. We call this radiation of energy that stems from the human spirit, our presence. This presence fills our physical bodies then our bodies magnify and project this energy into our physical world.

This is how the actions of our spiritual man are made manifest in the natural world. . Therefore, most Christians cannot manifest the miracle of healing by just speaking because their mode of operation contradicts their words. When God speaks of our ways, God is talking about our lifestyles and the way we operate in and out of Godliness frequently. The fruits of Godliness can't be manifested into the natural with a frequency that constantly changes.

That which is contemplated in that dark secret place speaking of our hearts will be revealed in the light through our actions. As we read and meditate constantly on the Word of God the Holy Spirit begins to fill our hearts by revealing Knowledge of Himself until we overflow. Until Christians discipline themselves to diligently study and meditate on God's Word to this point of overflow they will not see His Word manifest when they speak it. In Psalms 23 (TLB), when King David said my cup runs over he didn't mean that some of the contents of the cup were wasted. The cup symbolized David's heart that was overfilled with Revelation Knowledge of God until it issued out into his natural surroundings.

To achieve this overflow, one has to continually hear God speak into one's heart until they began to realize the sound, consistent, peace-filled climate of God's mind. Then God's demeanor will naturally overflow and be projected by their natural bodies into this present world. God is delivering us from our religious efforts of "faking it; until we get the manifestation" to the state of being the manifestation.

Through demonstration, our ways shape a form like a pantomime. As we speak our words begin to fill that form with the abundance of life that overflows from our hearts. This overflow from our hearts is what brings this form to life. Once alive we have a manifestation of whatever we have formed with our ways. Out of the abundance of our hearts flow the issues that manifest themselves in our lives. However, if the form that you demonstrate is different from the issue that is in your heart, the Word will not manifest when you speak it. This is because the form you are trying to demonstrate in the natural doesn't perfectly align with the issue that is in your heart. For example, on the outside, you might be smiling, but in your heart, you are wearing a frown. That smile on your face will not have any power behind it because the frown is the real issue of your heart. The issue of your heart is your spiritual energy that brings the form that you are demonstrating to life.

In this same manner if you display a frown on your face the issue of your heart empowers that negative form to manifest in the natural. . Others can now see, and feel, the effects of the negative manifestation. When we display a form contrary to the dominating issue of our hearts it is known as having a form of godliness. By only having the form of Godliness without a Godly heart leaves us incapable of filling the form we have on display. Therefore we put ourselves on display as Christians but we lack the power of God. Power can only be manifested externally when we have an abundant supply of it internally.

If our ways are evil ninety-nine percent of the time our cup will overflow with negative energy. As a result, we are powerless when it's time to heal the sick. Even though we put on an elaborate physical display of laying on of hands coupled with expressive speech our ineffectiveness is obvious. This is because the remaining one percent of Godliness lacks the volume needed to fill the form in order to manifest. God's grace is sufficient but living a sinful life on purpose and relying on grace, is like one who hears the Word and is not influenced by it. The Word of God says that this kind of person deceives himself. Manifestation comes from genuinely wanting to live Godly within your heart. When we fall short, grace takes over and fulfills our righteous intentions. This is not true for the opposite where you intentionally live a sinful life then expect grace to complete you.

Remember, God knows the intentions of our hearts and if our intentions are continually evil, God will not fulfill them. God is telling us that we can only manifest on the outside what we are on the inside. So, the good works and signs are not some exhibit that we are intentionally trying to display, but these manifestations come from just being who we are. A religious person can only display a form of Godliness, but only the person that has an abundance of Godliness in his heart can manifest that Godly power. When godliness is who you are it's easy to exhibit Godly qualities. God is bringing us out of the darkness of ignorance into the Light of His Knowledge so we can become the manifested Sons of God.

As we allow his Revelation knowledge to be poured out of His mind into our minds, it begins to flow over onto our flesh and is projected by our flesh into our daily lives. This overflow of oil that runs down our beards onto our bodies is the anointing. The signs of these supernatural manifestations will follow us automatically because of the excess of the Holy Spirit overflowing out from our lives onto the lives of others. This is how Jesus's Spiritual peace overflowed and took dominion over the situation that made His Disciples so distraught in the storm.

As a result of your knowing the steady, peaceful will of God, your overflow of the anointing in its manifested form, will engulf the people around you. The Power of the overflow of the Holy Spirit will be so evident that people will be healed by our shadows and by our residuals. When we get to this place of knowing God in our hearts, we won't be trying to demonstrate the manifestation we will be the manifestation. The Word of God tells us in John 1:12 (KJV) ***But as many as received him, to them gave them the power to become the sons of God, even to them that believe on his name.*** This power for kingdom manifestation is for the present. To achieve this level of power all of our ways have to acknowledge God, which means to accept his truth. When we accept His truth, we accept his sound, consistent mind. We build our faith on the solid rock of God's mind so that we can't be moved. Our ways will be unmovable and not easily given to emotions. This stable climate produces favorable conditions for the Tree of Life to grow within us.

This stable environment is the culture that the Children of God live by in the City of Truth, where the Name of the Lord is a Strong Tower. The Tower that stands there is a Tower of Praise edified by humility on the solid consistent foundation of the Revelatory Rock of the Word of God, which is Jesus Christ our Lord.

HOW TO CULTIVATE THE CULTURE

Remember these supernatural manifestations of the Spirit will not come because of what we try to be, but they will follow us just because of who we are. If you are a Son of God, you automatically do the things that your Father God does. You act the way He does. You respond to problems the way He does. You talk the way He does, you even begin to look at the world the way that He does. When we are filled from the inside out, which is God's order of operation that is so beautifully displayed by the rainbow; things begin to automatically take place because we are operating within his birth order. Nothing can come to pass outside of God's given law which is His Word. He is a God that holds His order or His Word above His name. Remember this Devine order of the Holy Trinity: the Father, the Son, and the Holy Spirit as you study the Word of God. With that being said, Satan's way is from the outside in. Satan walks around as an Angel of Light, displaying his false promise of wealth, telling the world that they can have these riches quickly with no regard for process. The process that Satan's system fails to consider is God's birth order. Satan's system offers one a quick profit if he or she bows down and worship's him. However, Satan the deceiver will not tell people of the sorrows that go along with these riches. These riches are on display in the lives of some of the most talented celebrities. These individuals have used their God-given gifts for themselves instead of using them to glorify God? The Word of God tells of how the sorrows of the people that utilize Satan's approach to riches eventually annul the glory of all their achievements. Satan strips them of everything by using cruel tactics that usually end in premature death. The destroyer then goes after their legacy utilizing any means necessary to annihilate anyone or anything attached to their name.

This is a sorrowful way to end but people still choose Satan's false light of immediate prosperity, rather than going through the process of Gods' birth order which is seed, time, and harvest. Even the Godly process of seed, time, and harvest has been misunderstood by man and the Church of Christ because of ignorance. The Church has been tricked into believing that after the seed of God's Word has been planted in their lives, there is nothing for them to do but live a cavalier life of the spirit while remaining totally oblivious to their carnal nature. As a result, Christians are disappointed and embarrassed when their carnal man entangles them in some kind of perverse sin. This form of Godliness lacks the power of God to resist the cravings of the carnal man acting as if he doesn't exist instead of confronting him.

The Bible says we must beat our flesh the same way Adam tilled the sin-cursed ground that our carnal man came from. If we don't do this, we are setting ourselves up for failure as we walk through life powerless as believers. The Bible says that the Kingdom of Heaven is on the inside of us where the flesh or our carnal man comes in contact with our spirit. The flesh has God-given virtues that it doesn't want to be exposed because of the callousness and stubbornness of sin. So like Adam, we must use the plow to turn the flesh inside out so that these virtues can be used by the Holy Spirit to manifest our Spiritual fruits in the natural. The only way God can carry out his plan on the earth is through our carnal man.

How do we cultivate the flesh or cultivate the culture? In Christianity cultivation is where the rubber meets the road or where carnality meets the Spirit It's at this point that you need to ask yourself if being a believer is going to be who you are or just a pretense? If you are going to be an authentic believer, it's time to sink the plow into your rebellious flesh and begin to overturn the soils of your carnal mind and never stop. Those who start to cultivate or renew their minds and turn back again to their old ways can't be used by the kingdom of God. The cultivation of our minds starts with this well-known scripture.

2 Chronicles 7:14 King James Version (KJV)
14 If my people, which are called by my name, shall humble themselves, and pray, and seek my face, and turn from their wicked ways; then will I hear from heaven, and will forgive their sin, and will heal their land.

In this passage, the God of all existence desires to restore His order to get the carnal man and earth back to His life-giving fruit of Wisdom. This life-giving fruit of Wisdom contains the Seed of the Knowledge of Truth. This Seed of Knowledge when planted in the cultivated soils of our renewed minds it gives birth to understanding. The understanding of believers now comes from the Holy Spirit that reveals the true knowledge of the written Word of God. Now we know not to allow our natural intelligence to dictate our decision-making because the natural mind was inherited from Satan in the Garden of Eden. This is the reason why we that have newly cultivated minds cannot rely on our own intelligence, but in ALL of OUR WAYS must reflect the light which is our insight from the mind of the Spirit

This principle of relying totally on God's Wisdom must be applied to always succeed in God's Will and not be led away by our own lusts. The fleshly mind is faulted like the plates of the earth and constantly comes into conflict with itself causing earthquakes, which represents, insta-bility, and leads to death. Death is a deterioration caused by separation from God. Our bodies, churches, and nations are deteriorating because we have separated ourselves from God. The deterioration of our land represents the fact that our souls, and bodies, are diseased. Our carnal man must be healed because the condition of our carnal man directly correlates with the condition of the dirt from which our carnal man was formed. As our flesh is healed Earth is healed also.

As the manifested sons of God, we are the epicenter of life for all of our connections. Our connections are our ancestors, siblings, offspring, neighbors, and the things we own. This is why all of God's dying cre-ation longs for believers to live a lifestyle that is governed totally by God's ordained principles. Once we propose in our hearts to become the sons of God intentionally, these manifestations of Godliness in our lives will reverse the curse of death off of ALL that choose life. The motivation to genuinely become a manifested son of God is realizing that the whole world is sick and dying and you have been given the power to heal it. However, when our ways are wicked we deny the power by blocking the path that the power of God needs to access the natural world. The intelli-gence that we purposefully choose to govern our lives whether Devine or carnal determines our outcome. These intentions of our hearts are what God observes from His standpoint of Humility. This humble view gives God a direct display of our motives allowing him to know the condition of our souls. All that are connected to us prosper as our soul prospers and the healing of our land starts with healing our souls.

God wants us to humble our carnal man with the plow of prayer and fasting. The plow symbolizes the discipline of our carnal man through sacrifice. Our carnal man abhors the pain of the plow but the health that permeates him as his soul and spirit man are enriched outweighs his carnal agony. This is the total opposite of the sorrow and pain that outweighs the pleasure of ill-gotten riches as previously stated.

As we endure the pain associated with the sacrifice of fasting we look to Jesus as our example like the Apostle Paul said in Hebrews 12:29 (KJV). Jesus is the author and finisher of our faith, *who FOR THE JOY that was set before Him endured the cross, despising the shame, and is set down at the right hand of the throne of God.*

What exactly are we doing when we fast? We are preparing the ground for worship or interaction with God through the process of turning over our old stubborn way of thinking represented by the thorns and thistle of the earth to expose the freshly cultivated soils of our new minds. The word wilderness is used to symbolize the humility that is necessary for sacrifice. God observing mankind from his throne at the center of humility calls for men to humble their hearts. Also from this standpoint in the wilderness, John the Baptist called for people to come and humble themselves in preparation for the Lord. As John prepared the way our Lord Jesus walked into the water to be baptized. Jesus is the seed of God's Word waiting to be planted into the newly cultivated mind. Baptism symbolizes the process of a seed being planted which is also in direct correlation with death and birth. Jesus being baptized represents burying the old man and the birth of a newborn. After this new birth, the Holy Spirit descends upon Jesus in the form of a dove symbolizing His total submission to the mind of the Spirit. Now under the direction of the Holy Spirit Jesus was led into the wilderness to fast for forty days and forty nights symbolizing that Jesus' carnal man was in total submission to His Spirit man. This tells us that the Son of God had to discipline his carnal man and we as sons of God must do the same. The disciplined carnal man not only listens to the mind of the Spirit but is submissive to do what the Spirit directs him to. The carnal mind that is humbled by fasting and prayer is ready for a joyful and powerful interaction between it and the Holy Spirit.

There have been numerous teachings on this subject, but most teachings fail to mention the virtues of the flesh. This lack of teaching on fleshly virtues probably stems from what Apostle Paul said about his carnal man in Romans 7:18 (KJV). In this passage, Paul tells us that nothing good can come from his fleshly man. He also explains that he has the desire to do good which means that he listens to the mind of the Spirit. Paul's dilemma was that His carnal man wouldn't carry out the Holy Spirit's desire. Later on in this passage, Paul mentions how he has to make the law of his carnal man a slave to the Law of the Holy Spirit. In 1 Corinthians 9:27 (KJV), Paul expounds further on how he has to make his carnal man a slave training it to do good things. What we should gain from Apostle Paul's teachings on the flesh is that the unconditioned flesh is not profitable. However, what we also learn is that the carnal man has good ethics within him that have to be worked out through discipline and conditioning. There are good fleshly virtues and gifts that God called "good" after He made man in his image. He instilled these virtues in man just like He instilled vitamins, and minerals into the black, moist soils of the earth. Fasting and prayer beat our carnal man under subjection forcibly opening his stubborn heart like a plow tilling the earth to expose its good God-given virtues.

Like a woman's womb, these soils are conducive to sparking growth and sustaining life. Before the sin of man, we learned in the book of Isaiah that like the womb of eve man's flesh and the earth gladly opened up before Adam to reveal the virgin soil. In this same manner, Adam's carnal man was receptive to Adam's spiritual man and they were both joined in a joyful union. Adam and Eve would have also enjoyed a joyful interaction of being joined in this manner. This joyful demonstration of praise by one willingly opening themselves to be fully known and joined with another is called worship. God connected us by creating us from the same substance. Adam, Eve, and Earth were connected because they were made from the same substance. The three of them were joined as one as the Father, Son, and Holy Ghost are one. This perfect connection of the Father, Son, and Holy Spirit is the order of God.

This is also the order of worship because this is the same way we open our minds to know God completely. In 2 Corinthians 9:6-7(KJV), the Apostle Paul writes about how one should give and the attitude of that giver. God loves cheerful givers, meaning the joyous feeling of giving must correspond with the Joy that is felt in knowing one's spouse in the act of worship. This act of worship is called sex.

God wants us to have this same willingness and joy whenever we give to Him. He never forces His way to our throne room located in the midst of our hearts where our treasures lie. Only Satan, the rapist would try to take control over the throne of our lives in that fashion. Jesus stands at the door and knocks. If anyone invites Him in, He will come in and dine with him. Jesus allows us to choose to crown him as the King of the throne room of our hearts.

Jesus' Spirit is a Gentleman that allows us to open the door to our hearts for Him. To open up means to cultivate. The original word cult before it was associated with the occult means to worship. The words cultivate means to prepare for worship. A cheerful giver opens up his or her heart gladly for the Holy Spirit. In this Joyful condition, the seed of God's knowledge is planted. When we overturn the soils of our minds, we expose our new minds while covering up our calloused old minds. This is a list of the Contrary Virtues associated with an old mindset that we are laying to rest:

> ***The Seven Contrary Virtues are pride, envy, gluttony, lust, anger, greed, slothfulness.***

Below are the good virtues that are being exposed so that the Holy Spirit can interact with us.

> ***These good virtues are faith, hope, charity, fortitude, justice, prudence, and temperance.***

THE TWELVE FRUITS OF THE SPIRIT

The first three of these seven virtues represent spiritual virtues. These three virtues symbolize the Devine Trinity, three in one, also known as God. The next four represent the four pillars: Abraham, Isaac, Jacob, and Esau. God didn't exclude Esau because of Jacob's Trickery but included everyone. Every time God and man interact God is magnified. Magnification is multiplication which means that when God's Spirit interacts with man's flesh a multiplicity of that interaction is manifested. Man was created to magnify God. . The sum of the three Godheads that make up the Devine Trinity multiplied by the four pillars equals twelve. Twelve is the number of the sons of Jacob. Each patriarch represents one of the twelve tribes of Israel. Jacob's sons also represent the twelve virtues of the flesh. Jacob's twelve sons have different roles based on the different blessings placed upon them by their father. These twelve sons also represent the realm of the Father or the written word. In the New Testament, Jesus's role is equivalent to Jacobs' in the Old Testament, and Jacob's twelve sons who symbolize the twelve virtues of the flesh also parallel with Jesus' twelve disciples who symbolize the twelve gifts of the Spirit. Jacob and Jesus both give birth to twelve sons, however, the twelve sons of Jacob are born of the flesh and the twelve sons of Jesus are born of the Holy Spirit. Each son of Jacob was given a stone that correlates with a fleshly virtue instilled into their carnal man by God. These different virtues directly affect the natural talents of a particular tribe of Israel. The twelve stones that are displayed on the ephod correspond with the rainbow of good carnal virtues inherited by man from God. Out of these different stones God birthed the great nation of Israel. As stated before the current nation of Israel was born of the flesh symbolizing that Jacob's sons were born of natural birth. Jesus' disciples who are fleshly descendants of these twelve tribes had to be born again of the Spirit. They too were given a stone as an inheritance but their stones represented Spiritual Virtues we call these Spiritual Gifts. These stones correlate with the rainbow of Spiritual Gifts of Light that are of the Holy Spirit. What makes these Spiritual Gifts so unique is that they need to interact with good carnal virtues in order to produce Spiritual Fruit. The physical must interact with the Spirit in order for Spiritual Fruit to manifest in the natural. Jacob and Jesus both begat the great nation of Israel; however, Jacob begat the physical nation of Israel while Jesus begat the new Spiritual nation of Israel. As with our carnal man Israel is still the same nation in the natural but it has to be born again into the Holy Spirit through Jesus Christ. Before this happens the Word of God tells us that the gentiles will have already begun the process of being added to the bloodline of these 12 tribes by accepting Jesus Christ as their Lord. Gentiles through the process of being born again will greatly multiply the census of Israel. As it is with our carnal man the result of Emmanuel being born to the nation of Israel and interacting with His people as a man resulted in the magnification of the nation of Israel. All of this took place because Jesus who is the seed of God fell upon good virtuous soils favorable for a Devine interaction and this was the Virgin Mary. Long before this seed was planted in the untouched virtuous womb of Mary a covenant symbolized by a stone was made between God and a man. A covenant or the joyful union of God and man always produces a seed. God made a covenant or a promise to an elderly man by the name of Abraham that He would give him a son. God fulfilled His promise to Abraham by giving Him a son but later God asked Abraham to sacrifice him. In obedience to God Abraham took his son Isaac to the place where God instructed him to carry out the Lord's request. God didn't allow Abraham to sacrifice his child but provided a ram to be sacrificed upon Mt. Moriah instead. Abraham dedicated this mountain or rock to the Lord by naming it "Jehovah Provides. Anything dedicated to the Lord in obedience is magnified and as a result, this rock became a symbol of the covenant God made to Abraham that He would give him many rocks or nations. This Mountain that now wore a new name is where the Temple of Jerusalem was built symbolizing the concealed covenant that God made with Abraham. This covenant will be revealed by the Holy Spirit to all who accept the blood of the lamb that was sacrificed there. This ram is the Lamb of God symbolizing Jesus that was sacrificed upon the rock God designated for Isaac. Now whoever accepts the Lamb of God accepts the bloodline of Abraham that was purified by Jesus's virtuous flesh coupled with the Gifts of the Holy Spirit making them heirs to the Throne of God. Being made the Children of God through this covenant means the seed of wisdom has been planted within us. In Revelation 22:2 (KJV), we read of a tree that bears twelve fruits every month for the healing of the nations. The seed of wisdom planted within us is the beginning of that tree. We must cultivate our minds to expose these twelve hidden virtues of the flesh to the twelve gifts of the Holy Spirit. Cultivation has to take place in order to produce the magnified twelve fruits of the Spirit. These twelve gifts are tools from the Holy Spirit needed to prepare these twelve good carnal virtues for use by transforming them into powerful Fruits of The Spirit. The twelve sons of Jacob represent the foundation or root system of this tree. Remember, the ground of our minds that we are cultivating has these twelve good virtues in it. The Word says that nothing good can come from the flesh. This means that nothing good can come from the flesh under its own authority. The flesh, like the topsoil of the earth, is hard and unyielding. The fleshly man is self-centered and gives no thought to the fact that he is a part of a three-part being. If your fleshly mind directs your life, you will not only die a physical death but you will also experience spiritual death. Spiritual death comes because your Spirit is separated from the nutrients it needs from the Word of God. The flesh is so selfish and greedy that it won't allow time for your Spirit man to eat of the bread of life. Instead, it's too busy living a life contrary to his good God-given virtues. As a result, the flesh becomes hardened towards the spirit and begins to manifest a very opinionated attitude toward life. The outcome of a fleshly governed life almost always ends in suicide; whether it is aggressive or passive suicide through issues such as over-eating, drug addiction, and taking a life-threatening risk. . These acts tell of a person that has little to no regard for life. It is similar to what Satan tried to tempt Jesus with when he told him to throw himself down from the high place where Satan had taken him. Jesus simply told Satan that it's not necessary to prove to mankind that I am the Son of God but for me to be the Son of God for mankind. God's power is not for us to prove what we can do through pride but for the power to do what is necessary through humility. Jesus knew it was necessary for the Son of God to give his life for mankind. The bottom line is that a prideful, carnally directed lifestyle ends in death. This is why Paul said nothing good can come from the flesh, but when the flesh is taken over and made to yield to the hands of our willing spirits we can overturn the opinionated wills of our minds to reveal their rich life-giving virtues. This is what the resurrection of Jesus symbolizes. It is the resurrecting of our minds back to God by revealing those good virtues that were covered by sin.

So when we fast, we are fasting against these contrary behaviors of the flesh by forcibly making it act the way it should and to do those things that are supposed to be done. While you're fasting, nothing should be able to offend you or change your attitude because you are operating in the good virtues. You fall short of glory whenever you stop plowing your ground and turn back to your old fleshly ways. The flesh loves food and drinks therefore sustenance should be one of the main areas of abstinence. Fasting is intentional and whatever is done for good intentionally, God graces and empowers it. While we fast we should stand steadfast on God's promises and our ways should be unmovable as we meditate on the Word of God. Do as the Apostles Paul said in *Ephesians 6:13-14 KJV; Having done all to stand Stand, therefore.* In other words continue to, plow.

Your objective while fasting is to train your flesh to continue operating in these good virtues even when your fast is finished. Dying by our own will to accept God's will with a joyful attitude should be our posture as we fast. If you give up your will angrily, then your fast is nothing more than a diet. God loves a cheerful giver so he reminds us to have a nice attitude towards others so that no one knows that we are fasting. However, be sensitive to the decent and orderly direction of the Holy Spirit as He leads you through this sensible path. You can always push yourself to do more but remember the purpose of a fast is to put those contrary virtues to rest without overstepping the boundaries. Do not kill your body trying to get it to submit, that would be murder. The disciplining of our carnal man is to break his will not to physically kill him. We break a stubborn horse for the purpose of using it. If we kill the horse during this process then how will it fulfill its purpose for us? Our carnal man can't fulfill his purpose of glorifying God on earth if he dies. God designed the carnal man so that His will can be done through mankind on earth. While fasting be responsible and take your prescription medicines and obey your physician. Jesus already paid the ultimate sacrifice and won so that we could live on and carry on his mission of reconciliation.

After we have prepared the soils of our minds through fasting and prayer, the next step is to seek God's face. Your quiet time before God during the process of fasting is when we gain more knowledge by reading and listening to the Word. We must purposefully prioritize our schedules around good, sound doctrine and Revelatory teaching. Radio and TV stations should be tuned to Christian teachings rather than music. Clear your mind of all your opinions while listening and reading the Word. As we have learned in prior chapters, your opinions are the carnal intellect that desires to suppress God's wisdom. While At this time, ask the Holy Spirit to give you His Wisdom. God's Wisdom is a direct thought from the mind of God the Father that He has sent or directed to your heart. Believers call these thoughts from God the Father to His children "Words of Wisdom". These Wise Words may be short but are complex in meaning. This is because God's thoughts are eternal in range and infinite in detail. It may take you or your descendant's several generations to live out the full details of a Word that God has put in your Heart. After you get a Word, God the Son will follow up with the evidence of that Word by confirming it with many written scriptures. God the Son also known as Jesus Christ came to earth so men may know or have evidence of God. This Word may still seem vague even after being validated by the Word of God. Before Jesus went to be with His Father He told his disciples that He had many things left to tell them but there wasn't enough time to explain eternity. Jesus stayed long enough to validate the Father's thoughts toward mankind so that mankind may believe in God. However, the whole purpose of seeking God is so we can understand Him. When we understand someone we not only have evidence of their existence but we also know them personally. God the Holy Spirit gives us an understanding of the Word by revealing who He is. He teaches you by breaking down the most complex thoughts of God so you can understand and relate to Him. This relationship with the Holy Spirit is gained by hearing and reading the Word, and also by asking the Holy Spirit for the meaning. This is how we meditate and seek God to know Him. The Holy Spirit can give understanding in many different ways. His answer may come by revealing it subconsciously. The Holy Spirit may also give answers through other passages of the Bible. At other times He may speak through the Pastor. However, once the response is given, it will be obvious that it was the Holy Spirit that gave the revelation because the answer is going to be tailored to how the question was asked.

As you become sensitive to the voice of the Holy Spirit an answer may come from a prerecorded message by a minister thousands of miles away This will strengthen your relationship with God when you realize that He answered your question several weeks in advance. This is a demonstration of how God answers before the question is asked. Ask the Holy Spirit for more of His wisdom, knowledge, and understanding as the relationship matures. As a consequence, trust is strengthened and all authority of the mind is given to God. Crowning Him over your mind results in your good virtues being exposed that influence a change in your ways.

Many Christians haven't matured to this point because they have never cultivated their minds in preparation to worship God in Spirit and truth. To prepare for this level of worship, Christians must realize that they and their entire livelihood belong to God. Withholding nothing by giving our all to God is a tough pill to swallow because many find their identities in their earthly affluence. The Word of God tells us that our very lives as Believers are not ours but has been paid for by the Blood of Him who gave His all for us on Calvary's cross. Everything was given to men on this earth by God and nothing is theirs to keep, but it is only a gift given to them so that they can give it to others.

Acts 20:35 KJV
35 I have shewed you all things, how that so labouring ye ought to support the weak, and to remember the words of the Lord Jesus, how he said, It is more blessed to give than to receive.

As believers, we must mature to the area of willful reformation from the inside out, not as mere performers but as manifested sons of God.

This is a power-infused lifestyle of unconditional love that naturally generates signs and wonders on the earth. This leads us to our next step in the process of cultivation. By preparing the way for the Lord we are preparing our individual temples or our bodies to receive the Holy Spirit.

Once we get our houses in order (fleshly bodies) then we must turn from our wicked movable ways. Isn't it interesting that God would want us to change our mode of operation or the way we portray things? Up until now, Christians have been manifesting a lifestyle contrary to their title, thus becoming the hypocrites Isaiah prophesied about. Jesus said in Matthew 15:8-9 (KJV),

8This people draws near to me with their mouth, and honors me with their lips; but their heart is far from me. 9But in vain they do worship me, teaching for doctrines the commandments of men.

God wants us to live our lives from the inside out, rather than the outside in. This is his principle of humility that is reflected in every little aspect of God's kingdom. In the middle is where He resides and from that perspective is how he operates. Anything that doesn't operate in that order is out of order and will not bear fruit. Life always begins for man in his smallest form as a seed in the midst of a woman and so it is with the kingdom of Heaven. Mark 4:26 (NKJV) says, *So is the kingdom of God, as if a man should cast seed into the ground.* This represents God's principle of humility where power is birthed. The word of God constantly alludes to this place of humility as the Tree of Life in the center of the Garden. God wants to teach us how to live our lives from the inside out because the Kingdom of God is inside of us and it has to be manifested by our ways. Not by trying in the form of an act but because of who we are. God wants us to bring forth fruit of ourselves like the earth.

Mark 4:28 (KJV) 28For the earth bringeth forth fruit of herself; first the blade, then the ear, after that the full corn in the ear.

God is saying that what is planted inside you will eventually outgrow everything else until it takes over all your thoughts in the garden of your mind. Then in the fullness of time, you will bear much fruit that will be so plentiful that they manifest themselves automatically through your ways.

This is the same principle of humility that Jesus spoke about in the parable of the mustard seed. "The Kingdom of Heaven is like a mustard seed that someone planted in his field; it is the smallest of all the seeds, but when it has grown it becomes a tree so that the birds come and make nests in its branches. This standpoint of humility ultimately puts you in a position of power that comes from within. In other words, you have become just like the tree that was planted by the rivers of water that bring forth his fruit in his season. Remember, whatever you plant in your mind is what you become as that governing tree takes hold of your thought process. This is where the next principle comes into action and that principle is whatever a man thinks in his heart, so is He. The objective of being a believer is to allow the seed of knowledge to mature to the point that all your ways reflect the will of that tree. So now the fruit that you bear which are the manifested gifts of the Spirit will give life to others. The sons and daughters of God grow from the inside out and when they mature they will bear much fruit. This is the reason the Pharisees were powerless. They were looking for an external kingdom that only could be found internally.

The Kingdom of Heaven is found on the inside. It's those good virtues that currently exist in the soils of your mind that you bring out by seeking God's knowledge through prayer and fasting. These virtues were there all the time but were covered by the stubbornness of the carnal will because of sin. These good virtuous soils that lie beneath the calloused will of the carnal mind are elements of the Kingdom of Heaven that Jesus spoke of in his reply to the Pharisees in Luke 17:20-21

Luke 17:20-21 ESV
20 Being asked by the Pharisees when the kingdom of God would come, he answered them, "The kingdom of God is not coming in ways that can be observed, 21 nor will they say, 'Look, here it is!' or 'There!' for behold, the kingdom of God is in the midst of you."

The Kingdom of Heaven is presently in the place that God's principle of humility said it would be: in our core patiently waiting for the stone that was appointed by God to turn these hidden virtues into manifested fruit. This authorized stone is the Seed of Knowledge. The seed of knowledge can only be found in the midst of the fruit of Wisdom that is produced by the Tree of Life.

The seed of knowledge that comes from seeking the Lord is the only seed that produces roots strong enough to pierce the soils of the carnal mind and utilize those core elements (virtues) to establish a firm understanding. Planted in the carnal mind, the seed will continue to grow as long as the person continues to seek God's Wisdom and receive it with a glad heart. When the tree reaches a certain level of maturity, the carnal mind of a man will resemble the tree that abides within Him. When this happens we begin to produce fruit naturally because we begin to acknowledge God in all that we do. Once one reaches this stage in the process one has become a manifested son of God.

The Pharisees had no fruit to show because they didn't have the tree that produces the fruit planted on the inside. Until Believers learn to teach what is necessary to produce spiritual growth on the inside and not focus on how believers should appear on the outside, they will continue to be powerless. What is necessary to produce fruit is not in our skillful acts. How eloquently we preach or how we dress are all vain external displays but true power comes from within. However, if we're not humbling ourselves and cultivating our ground to prepare for interaction with the Father, we cannot expect to receive the seed of knowledge that grows into Godly Wisdom. Without this knowledge, we are portraying a form of Godliness like a character in a superhero movie. As believers, we have on the suit and cape but we can't fly because we don't have the power.

As a result, we as believers are not productive in the immediate healing of our loved ones. This lack of power proves its ineffectiveness even when the conditions are favorable and the people are desperate in their belief that the power of the Holy Spirit can heal them. . Believers are powerless because they portray or manifest a form but like a dam in a river they have hindered the power it takes to fill that image by not preparing their flesh which is the path the Holy Spirit must take into their natural lives. As long as the believers' carnal man hasn't been disciplined by his spirit to the place that his carnal ways line up with his spiritual will then the road for the Lord is not ready. John the Baptist said, "make a straight path for the Lord to travel". The path that the Holy Spirit takes must be straight meaning that your spirit's desire must be in line with His and your fleshly ways must be trained to do what your spirit says. All of our carnal ways must acknowledge our spiritual will and the will of our spirit man must line up with the Holy Spirit. In this same perfect alignment are the paths between the Father, Son, and Holy Spirit, and this same path must be made straight for these three beings to travel as one Deity into our natural world. God's will and His Kingdom can only come through us in our present lives through the disciplining of our carnal man. When all of the motives of our souls, spirits, and bodies are in perfect alignment with His will the Holy Spirit immediately fills our forms manifesting His will on earth.

This brings us to our next step which is God hearing His Words from Heaven spoken out of our mouths then watching over His Words to perform them. When God knows you as His son He will not let his Word return void. Then, he heals your flesh and all that is connected to it, which includes your land.

What is God hearing from Heaven? God is hearing the cry from the hearts of his people who are now close to him instead of the distant cries from the lips of the hypocritical Pharisees. Jesus spoke about this in Matthew *15:8 (NIV), These people honor me with their lips, but their hearts are far from me.*

God desires to reconcile man's mind back to Himself. This is the connection the mind of God shared with the mind of Adam in the Garden of Eden. The minds of God and Adam were connected as one as in marriage. This is the reason why we go through the painful process of cultivating our minds. Like a Bride prepares for her Groom, in that same manner we prepare for interaction with God. Once, we have opened our hearts to draw near unto God through praise, He in return draws nigh unto us. God's objective is to know our hearts. In other words, God's will is to know the desires of our hearts. This is the same heart that He couldn't know before because our thoughts were evil, and the side effect of evil thoughts is a closed heart towards God. Since we have cultivated our minds so that they display to God only those Good virtues that He placed within us our desires are now aligned with His will. Our will for God is for Him to heal our flesh and all of its connections.

Jesus came so that all of creation through him might be saved and healed. When observing God's will and our desires, they should be one and the same. His will for us is to prosper and be in Good health. He heals our land and gives us the desires of our hearts because God knows we are delighted to receive him like a woman who is delighted to be with her husband.

Psalms 37:4 (ESV) Delight yourself in the LORD,
and he will give you the desires of your heart.

The place of perfect peace is what is being described in Psalms 37:4. This is a place that can only be found at the center of our hearts. This was the place that was in Jesus' heart that allowed him to sleep on the stormy sea. This was the same area of green pastures where David was made to lie down allowing God to restore his soul. David also found security and counsel in this area as God prepared a table for him in the presence of his enemies. In this setting, David did not need to fear for his life because God's rod and staff comforted him. This place is the Kingdom of Heaven that is found within the hearts of those who truly desire to let the Seed of Knowledge grow at the center of their hearts.

This is a soul ablaze with the glory of God that originates from the fertile soils of humility and illuminates the human spirit. The light of our spirit man then radiates through the body like a lamp overflowing with the power of the Holy Spirit changing everything and everyone it touches. The Kingdom that resides in us is a place that has been prepared and reserved only for the sons of God. Within this place is a peace that surpasses all understanding. How do we enter such a place? We enter this place through rest.

Hebrews 4:11 YLT
May we be diligent, then, to enter into that rest, that no one in the same example of the unbelief may fall.

We must be diligent in cultivation because we are always turning over more ground daily to receive a harvest. This Heavenly place is why we labor for six days out of the week so that we can enter into this place of Heavenly interaction and worship. This secret area is a place of delight where the seed of the Word of God is planted in our hearts. This description of the secret place of God poetically portrays its beauty. God is saying that the Church assembly represents the place of sabbatical rest that we must enter and have interaction with God. We have to diligently work to prepare for worship on a daily basis. Then at some point during the day we need to have a one on one time of reading and seeking God's face to know Him better. We must seek Him diligently as we mature by keeping our minds constantly focused on the Lord and He, in turn, will keep us in this area of perfect peace. If you enter this secret place on a daily basis, you will know where to take refuge in times of trouble. We shouldn't fear the storm because we know whose we are and where we are in Him. We are God's sons and the Kingdom of Heaven is every-where we are because it resides in us.

This behavior may seem strange in the same manner that Jesus was perceived by His disciples as he slept on the boat. However, this area of Heaven was realized in the eyes of his disciples when Jesus manifested that sound supernatural environment of perfect peace within him by speaking it. The disciples began to talk among themselves saying this really is the Son of God.

We must realize that we are little Kingdoms of Heaven walking around on this earth. Like earth and Heaven, we have a magnetic core which is our soul, a mantle which is our Spirit, and a crust which is our flesh. Our core affects the energy felt around the outside of our body, which is our attitude. We must radiate or project a constant attitude of Joy. This is what people feel when they are close to each other.

Diligent one on one time with God causes you to have a consistent atmosphere. This reflects that you have a good core of understanding which is the rock on which your foundation is established. Each heart in an assembly of saints should manifest a consistent peaceful climate collectively. This spiritual energy stems from the core of the Sons of God who carry the Kingdom of Heaven within their hearts. The church is a physical manifestation of the place of rest that each Son of God individ-ually worked to enter. Now after six days of diligent work individually, they assemble to praise God as one body corporately. This atmosphere of praise is where God desires to abide. Then as the seed of the Word is planted miracles are birthed. The Church of Jesus Christ should be the physical manifestation of a place of perfect peace. In this place, there is no complaining because each son of God has humbled himself by cultivating his soil to manifest the desire of the Holy Spirit. This happens as we do our parts in completing each other instead of competing with one another. Our integrity is also paramount in being able to worship God in Spirit and Truth.

Philippians 2:12-15 KJV
12 Wherefore, my beloved, as ye have always obeyed, not as in my presence only, but now much more in my absence, work out your own salvation with fear and trembling.

13 For it is God which worketh in you both to will and to do of his good pleasure.

14 Do all things without murmurings and disputings:

15 That ye may be blameless and harmless, the sons of God, without rebuke, in the midst of a crooked and perverse nation, among whom ye shine as lights in the world.

When we intentionally dwell within that extension of the Kingdom of Heaven in our hearts, our whole lifestyle should change or conform to the culture of the Kingdom of Heaven. **Psalm 91 King James Version (KJV)**

---

91 He that dwelleth in the secret place of the most High shall abide under the shadow of the Almighty.

If a specific culture fascinates you to the point that you desire to move to that country to make that civilization your new lifestyle that is how your desire should be as it pertains to the culture of the Kingdom of Heaven. As you live with God inside this Heavenly Kingdom, He begins to show you His ways of wisdom which lead to abundance in every area of life: Spirit, Soul, Body, Social, and Financial. As you conform, you will see your whole life transform into what God has shown you within your Heart. Now the power to manifest God's desire on earth comes naturally. Besides, you'll have freedom in knowing that you don't have to act like a Believer because a Believer is who you are.

Whatever nationality you are from, you don't have to use any extra energy trying to tell others that you are from that particular nation. Others will automatically notice your unique differences as you interact with them. Your accent and other things exclusive to your culture will identify your ethnicity.

In Ephesians 4:1-3(TLB), the Apostle Paul begs the church of Ephesus to conform to the distinctive character traits specific to the culture of the Kingdom of Heaven. Some of the traits given are humility, gentleness, and patience.

Ephesians 4: 1-3 Living Bible (TLB)
4 I beg you—I, a prisoner here in jail for serving the Lord—to live and act in a way worthy of those who have been chosen for such wonderful blessings as these. 2 Be humble and gentle. Be patient with each other, making allowance for each other's faults because of your love. 3 Try always to be led along together by the Holy Spirit and so be at peace with one another.

As Paul stated, under the utterance of the Holy Spirit, humility is the root of our unique character traits as Kingdom citizens. Then from humility comes love. A proud person cannot love; they can only do those things that are contrary to what Paul wrote from prison to the Church in

Ephesus. Mean-hearted, nasty, vindictive, slanderous, gossiping believers are a result of a lack of proper cultivation. These contrary virtues represent the hard soils and the rebellious thorns and thistles of Satan. Jesus told us how to identify the traits of humble, well-disciplined Believers:

John 13:35 NIV
By this everyone will know that you are my disciples, if you love one another.

What you should see taking place in your life is that you are being reconciled back to that Eden lifestyle that Adam and Eve lived naturally. Your habits should reflect those habits of Adam and Eve because of God ordering your decision process. This lifestyle change will naturally cause you to live a longer more abundant life on earth. Jesus is the seed of the Knowledge of God's Wisdom that is planted in our hearts enabling us to possess abundant life as an inheritance. This seed germinates within us as we seek God to know Him and become accustomed to His lifestyle. As this seed becomes a tree within us our natural man begins to manifest the fruits from this tree into the natural. We begin to live more abundantly as we walk out of our new lifestyle that produces the climate our tree needs to be productive. Now as a result of others consuming our produce they can live as well. As the people who benefit from the life-giving sustenance of our fruit genuinely believe, the seed from our fruit is planted in their hearts as well. Also, those who eat our manifested fruits will be healed, delivered, and made whole. These will be the signs that follow those who believe.

To know or see our father just as He is, means to know Him as He knows himself. Your kin, those connected to you, and those that live with you in your household know your ways. Your children know you by learning your habits and unique characteristics. They understand and know what makes you happy, mad, or sad. They even know how you feel about certain issues and topics. Your children develop these same characteristics, habits, and insights because they have been molded by you. Now we see what Jesus is saying when he says I only do what I see my Father does and no one knows the Father but His son. Jesus told his disciples if you have seen me, you have seen the Father. This is how God wants the manifestations of the Sons of God to be on the earth. If people look upon you and see anything other than God, then you are manifesting the image and likeness of Satan. Satan's pride working in us is the reason we as humans would rather go to nightclubs and dance, to draw attention to ourselves. Not only is this pride found in nightclubs, but in places of business, governments, and even in the Church of the Living God. Why do men need Satan's pride that causes competition between themselves to have a sense of self-worth? Satan set this system of competitive pride in place so he could magnify his throne over God by getting man to bring worship to himself instead of God. Man's flesh wants the approval of others; this is the only way to achieve self-worth in Satan's system of Pride.

Like the Tower of Babel was built as a testament to man, in this day in time man has made a golden calf of himself. The current lifestyle of musicians has become a testament to themselves bragging about how well they live and the things they possess. The fans have become worshipers of celebrities' talents and beauty and desire it for themselves. Entertainers compete for the worship of fans to the point that they feud and write rude lyrics about the other artist to steal their worshipers.

Satan's system of pride requires them to do this so that they may find their esteem in the riches they gain. This is the way Satan does God. The only thing is, God is not in a competition for worshipers like Satan. Instead of the spotlight of wealth and fame, God disguises his True light with the darkness of humility. Rather than being the feature in a public setting, God wants us to seek him in the humble secret place called the Holy of Holies of our hearts. If we do this as the Word of God says in *Matthew 6:4(KJV)and thy Father which seeth in secret himself shall reward thee openly.* This is also done in prayer :

Matthew 6:6 KJV
But thou, when thou prayest, enter into thy closet, and
when thou hast shut thy door, pray to thy Father which
is in secret; and thy Father which seeth in secret shall
reward thee openly.

From God's standpoint of humility, we are required as worshipers in the system of praise to be planted in secret in order to be exalted in public. This is why we have such a struggle between people in the church. They don't realize that their gifts make room for them not them making room for their gifts. We let our gifts make room for us by humbling ourselves as was represented by Joseph. Joseph remained humble in prison until a door was opened in Pharaoh's palace for his gift. According to God's design, no one had the gift to interpret Pharaoh's dream but Joseph's. The gift that a person doesn't possess, is what opens the door for your gift in their lives. . Joseph's spiritual gift for the interpretation of dreams coupled with his natural talent for administration gave him favor with the Pharaoh. As a result, Joseph was given a new name, a wife, and a new position of prominence as the Prince of Egypt. Joseph's new highly esteemed position ultimately allowed him to fulfill his God-given childhood dream and purpose. God's gift may not make you successful overnight as Satan's claims do, but if you are willing to be humble and wait God will exalt you with great rewards.

Until we understand within the church which represents the heart of the people, we will always use our gifts to compete with another's gifts out of pride, instead of waiting and letting our gift make room for us. If we are prideful our pride is hurt when someone seems to be more gifted and noticed by the leadership of the church. This is a result of the satanic system of pride. The root cause of us being hurt or offended is that we esteem ourselves on being recognized. Then, when that need for recognition is not fulfilled our self-image deflates. Our self-worth should come from God within us and not from the external world around us.

However, if pride was not a factor in the house of God the feelings that come with rejection and promotion would be mutual. At the feet of humility, your self-esteem can't be lowered by rejection and it can't be exalted by promotion. Since we have already placed ourselves in a lowly position in God we don't feel the pain in rejection. While having this same demeanor we won't be prideful in a promotion. Humility does this by keeping us from esteeming ourselves more highly than we ought to. As a result of humility, we maintain consistent well-mannered attitudes resulting in a peaceful atmosphere within the church. When it comes to positions of prominence in the church our natural instinct is to jump at the opportunity only to fall painfully on the floor of rejection. Pride comes before a fall so keep your feet planted on God's foundation of humility. When faced with negation remember the stone that the builders of the Church reject will become the keystone. God will bring our gifts to the front if we keep ourselves in the back.

Being rejected should be first nature to a Believer because we are humbled like Jesus who was rejected numerous times yet still did what he had to do for the people who rejected him. Digging down and seeking God to know him is how God is building his tower of praise stone by stone.

THE TOWER OF PRAISE

Your stone is alive. When God is speaking of your stone, He is speaking of the stone of life that He has given you as an inheritance. The ancient Hebrews gave stones to their children for them to remember what God had brought their people through. Also, this stone is the rock-solid word of God that is written on the stone tablets of our hearts. This stone represents the solid, steadfast love of God inherited by man but now has become stone-cold by Adam's rebellion. God started transforming man's stubborn heart of stone back into a steadfast position by breaking up its foundation revealing the fountains of His Word as in the flood of Noah.

Proverbs 3:18-20 TLB

18 Wisdom is a tree of life to those who eat her fruit; happy is the man who keeps on eating it.

19 The Lord's wisdom founded the earth; his understanding established all the universe and space. 20

The deep fountains of the earth were broken open by his knowledge, and the skies poured down rain.

God revealed the deep fountains hidden in our stony, stubborn hearts that represent those good virtues that He placed in us. Out of this rock, water flows and springs up within us into eternal life. Wisdom, knowledge, and understanding flow from this rock down to us as it does out from the base of Mt Hermon forming the Jordan River. As these waters flow downward through History these same life-giving waters were seen gushing from the rock that Moses struck rather than speaking to as God had instructed. Moses hit the rock representing his rebellious heart and the people's hearts. As a result, they couldn't enter The Promised Land.

The third chapter of Proverbs gives the direct opposite of a stony rebellious heart. It refers to the good pliable hearts of men which allow this tree of Wisdom to be planted in them. We allow this tree to be planted within our hearts by doing what is written in Hosea 10:12 NIV:

Hosea 10:12 New Living Translation
I said, 'Plant the good seeds of righteousness, and you will harvest a crop of love. Plow up the hard ground of your hearts, for now, is the time to seek the LORD, that he may come and shower righteousness upon you.'

If we follow these steps of humility, the seed of wisdom will enter our hearts located at the center of our beings allowing the kingdom of Heaven to take root within us. This is stated in Proverbs 2:10.

Proverbs 2:10 TLB
10 For wisdom and truth will enter the very center of
your being, filling your life with joy.

As with Mt Hermon, a river of water flows out of the Living Stone which represents the heart. This living water is the living Word. As the living word fills our hearts we become overwhelmed to the point that we are overflowing with unspeakable joy. Joy is the atmosphere of the Kingdom of Heaven. In 1Peter 1:8 -9, it speaks of this joy that can't be explained.

1Peter 1:8-9 TLB
8You love him even though you have never seen him.
Though you do not see him now, you trust him; and
you rejoice with a glorious, inexpressible joy. 9The
reward for trusting him will be the salvation of your
souls.

The Joy of the Lord is the strength that surrounds and shields us like the earth's atmosphere does for it. Joy is the ambiance that protects us from the evil energies that bombard us in order to forcefully enter the Heavenly Kingdom of our hearts. .We declared our hearts to be Heavenly Kingdom territory by accepting Jesus the Seed of Wisdom. By accepting this seed we allowed the Tree of Life to be planted in the fertile soils of our minds. At the center of the Garden of our minds this tree begins to sprout as its roots grow to overtake the soils that govern our thoughts. God's inexpressible joy is our reward for entrusting the Kingdom of Heaven to protect us and govern our lives. Joy surrounds this Heavenly Kingdom founded upon a rock known as the Seed of Wisdom that was planted in the place designated by God at the center of our hearts.

Our joy gives us the strength to stand against troubling spirits like the earth's atmosphere protects it from foreign objects. However, these spirits desire to overtake our joy by bombarding us with their many troublesome methods. For example one of the most successful ways Satan overtakes us is by fear. The spirit of fear pounds its way through our atmosphere forcing its way into our midst. If this spirit can infiltrate its evil energy into the soils of your mind it can alter your consistent Godly thought pattern troubling your heart. This weakens you, causing you to yield to its control as it overtakes you. God didn't give us the spirit of fear but of love, power, and a sound mind. The Joy of the Lord is our first line of defense against Hell's forces. The Word of God says that the Heavenly Kingdom within our hearts suffers violence and our many violent adversaries desire to take over the central government of our hearts by force. Our enemy uses intimidation in hopes that we withdraw our trust from Jesus who is the King of our hearts and rely upon our carnal understanding for instruction. When we stop trusting in King Jesus for our protection we override His commands by taking back control over the central government of our hearts. As we withdraw from trusting in the Lord's Word His impervious atmosphere of inexpressible Joy is inhibited leaving us open for attack. We suffer at the hands of our violent enemies because we withdraw ourselves from God's knowledge. Each man opens the door welcoming his own suffering because of his own lack of Heavenly instruction.

The lord over these forces that constantly come against us is Satan, who is still trying to force his way into the Kingdom of God from the outside. If Satan can take our focus off of God then he can take what is ours. Hence we must protect our hearts from the terrors we see, hear, and feel by keeping our trust in God which gives us Joy and brings us peace.

John 14:27 King James Version (KJV)
27 Peace I leave with you, my peace I give unto you: not
as the world giveth, give I unto you. Let not your heart
be troubled, neither let it be afraid.

John 14:27 (KJV) not only speaks of peace as it pertains to war but this passage also speaks of peace from noisome interference. This is a peace that blocks out all the interference that is flying through our atmosphere that Satan uses to keep us from hearing the voice of God. In Matthew 16:18 (ESV), Jesus speaks of this noisy interference as the "gates of Hell". The Latin translation for the word "gate" is the word bab which means noise. Earlier in this same chapter, Jesus asked his disciples "who do men say that I am"? His disciples replied to Jesus with several responses that are recorded in that biblical text. These many responses and theories that different men were thinking represent the noisy interference from Hell designed to distort the true revelation of Jesus from their minds. After this Jesus asked his disciples "who do you say that I am"? Simon responded to Jesus by saying "you are the Son of God". This was evidence that Simon had blocked the noisy interference from men influenced by evil spirits only to hear the still small voice of God. The voice of God, Jesus' Father, had revealed this knowledge unto Simon giving him the same inheritance from the Father that Jesus had. This inheritance was the rock of the covenant that God made with Abraham. This rock came with a new identity, a new purpose, and a new name. The rock's name was Peter and the noisy interference from Hell could not prevail against it.

Instead

Matthew 16:18 ESV
18 And I tell you, you are Peter, and on this rock[a] I
will build my church, and the gates of hell[b] shall not
prevail against it.

Jesus lets us know what produces a constant atmosphere of Joy in this verse; which is a sound mind and heart coming from the rock of the revealed Word of the Father. This rock is Jesus that gives Peter the perfect peace as stated in John 14:27(KJV) that fills his heart with joy overflowing from his core, forming an atmospheric force field of strength and protection around him. This overflowing joy was also found at the Church of Macedonia in the face of severe persecution.

"And now, brothers and sisters, we want you to know
about the grace that God has given the Macedonian
churches. In the midst of a very severe trial, their over-
flowing joy and their extreme poverty welled up in rich
generosity." 2 Corinthians 8:1-2 NIV

It all begins and ends at the living rock known as the Kingdom of Heaven that is in our hearts. Jesus is at the core of it all in the center of the rainbow and on the throne of hearts. Out of this rock flows the issues of our lives. If our hearts are stable, then our atmosphere is stable. If we keep our focus on seeking His face; others can see the light of God's joyous countenance shining through our atmosphere. In this same respect, we observe Moses who out of anger struck this rock with his staff instead of speaking to it, and from that rock flowed the issue that kept him from entering the Promised Land. Like Moses, if our hearts are troubled, then the stormy clouds of our sadness, bitterness, and anger cover the Lord's bright countenance. When our clouds overcast God's countenance we are exalting our emotions over the Light of God's promises. As a result, people can only see and feel the bad vibes of our contrary atmosphere. In this same manner, Lucifer tried to block out God's light and exalts himself over God. This would be a test of faith as in:

James 1:2-4 ESV
2 Count it all joy, my brothers,[a] when you meet trials of various kinds, 3 for you know that the testing of your faith produces steadfastness. 4 And let steadfastness have its full effect, that you may be perfect and complete, lacking in nothing.

To be steadfast and unmovable means to be as unmovable as a stone. Don't mistake this for being hardheaded and stubborn, which is just the opposite of being steadfast. Being headstrong is one of the main contrary sinful traits of Satan. Instead, be firm, making sure your focus is always on God and determined not to let the troublesome cares and worries disrupt our peaceful and joyous Kingdom atmosphere. Let the strength of your joy ward off the fiery asteroids or darts of Satan by keeping your faith focused on God as Paul the Apostle. The shield of faith is just one of the six different layers of defense in our atmosphere of Joy. These layers just like the different invisible layers of the earth's atmosphere, ward off and absorb many schemes of Satan on a daily basis.

Earth's atmosphere protects the earth from asteroids that could do considerable damage to the earth and its inhabitants. This is the unseen realm of earth, like the spirit of man that experiences what he doesn't see with his fleshly eyes. Like the earth, we are a solid rock with a fiery core. Within our fiery core, our souls are the Governing Throne of God. This Throne room is the center of Government for our three-part being. In addition to the core which represents our soul the earth's mantle and crust are our spirit and body. The way the invisible energy of the earth radiates out of its crust is in direct correlation with how the human spirit issues out of the carnal man. Like the Holy Spirit that searches the heart of God to know His Mind and dwells within the Son our human spirit knows our mind and resides in our bodies. As a result of our human spirit knowing our hearts, our spiritual energy which extends beyond our carnal man manifests our mood into the natural. In this same manner, the earth's core energy determines our daily weather. This spiritual energy brings whatever our hearts or minds have thought of in the form of facial expressions or movements that we call body language.

This is how the thoughts of our hearts are manifested into the physical realm. These motions and actions build a spiritual form like a concrete layer builds a form in the shape of what he wants. After the form is built, the concrete that represents the spirit in this case then fills the hollow space manifesting the form.

As a result of our spirit man, the condition on the inside of our hearts has now become our condition on the outside. God told us; it is not by might nor by power but by His Spirit. We are made in God's image and likeness so our three beings were created to operate just like God. We've had our human spirit since birth, but if we are born again the Holy Spirit now dwells within our hearts and minds forming a union of our human spirit and the Holy Spirit as in a marriage. This is how the spiritual energy of the earth manifests because He that dwells or lives in the heart and mind of the earth automatically knows what is going on.

This is the same with our physical house because we live inside of them; we automatically know what's going on. If the mood in your physical house is happy, the world will know because of the way you interact with people. If your facial expression doesn't give you away, your spiritual energy or vibe will. You can meet a person and they greet you with a smile, but their vibes let you know they have a frown internally. . What you felt is that person's spirit which is a reflection of how that person actually feels in his or her heart. Your ability to feel this vibe has its roots in a gift called spiritual discernment. The Spirit knows the heart and mind because it dwells in them.

Romans 8:27 NIV
27And he who searches our hearts knows the mind of the Spirit because the Spirit intercedes for God's people in accordance with the will of God.

This scripture of course is speaking of the Holy Spirit who Jesus has sent to lead, guide, and guard us.

John 16:13 Good News Translation
When, however, the Spirit comes, who reveals the truth about God, he will lead you into all the truth. He will not speak on his own authority, but he will speak of what he hears and will tell you of things to come.

We were once connected to God's fire of truth, which protected us by seeing into our future and telling us of things to come. Since we live in a fallen world, God has given us the Holy Spirit our comforter to cover and protect us. He who surrounds us is also within us protecting us from the world around us.

John 4:4 KJV
Ye are of God, little children, and have overcome them:
because greater is he that is in you, than he that is in
the world.

Adam and Eve had the light of the truth that surrounded them like the earth's atmosphere. This light was man's spirit that was directly connected to God's Wisdom. Man's Spirit was illuminated with the light of the truth that beamed from the solid rock of the Wisdom of God. This rock was directly connected to the understanding of God's Truth, provided by His Holy Spirit, the fiery core foundation found inside the stable mind of Adam and Eve. This caused their spirits to glow with the Wisdom, Knowledge, and understanding of God's truth that was noticeable on the outside of their bodies. This Fire of The Spirit of Truth clothed them before sin, hence they never saw their bodies as being naked until after sin. Disconnected from The Spirit of God, man's spirit lost its light because The Fire of the Spirit of Truth was no longer with them.

Now through Jesus, the Holy Spirit can once again illuminate men and women with His knowledge and understanding of their Father God. His light is the life of all men. In turn, this gives man the power to know God as His Son Jesus knows Him. This knowledge of the Father gives them the power to become the manifested Sons of God lit with the Fire of God's Truth.

Lit with the joyous atmosphere of the Holy Spirit, God's Truth in love starts at the most humble place in our hearts then extends outward to protect us from all the wiles of Satan. Just like the earth's atmosphere extends upwards from its core the atmosphere of our spirit, now inhabited by the Holy Spirit, extends from our bodies upwards into eternity. This high place is where the Apostle Paul says we wrestle with principalities, powers, and all sorts of spiritual wickedness. These evil entities want to rule over the high places of our spirit, just like they rule over the earth's atmosphere. They do this in order to hinder you from receiving the manifestation of God like they did Daniel. However, the Greater one who lives on the inside of us has provided us with layers of defense, just like the different layers of Earth's atmosphere. Apostle Paul described these layers as different pieces of Armor. Since we are speaking of high places of the Spirit let's start reading there.

Ephesians 6:11-17 (KJV) 11Put on the whole armor of God, that ye may be able to stand against the wiles of the devil. 12For we wrestle not against flesh and blood, but against principalities, against powers, against the rulers of the darkness of this world, against spiritual wickedness in high places. 13Wherefore take unto you the whole armor of God, that ye may be able to withstand in the evil day, and having done all, to stand. 14Stand therefore, having your loins girt about with truth, and having on the breastplate of righteousness; 15And your feet shod with the preparation of the gospel of peace; 16Above all, taking the shield of faith, wherewith ye shall be able to quench all the fiery darts of the wicked. 17And take the helmet of salvation, and the sword of the Spirit, which is the word of God:

Our lines of defense are in direct correlation with the order of God. First in line is the Sword of the Spirit which is the Word of God. Hearing the Word of God brings faith. Next in line is the shield of Faith because before you can be saved, you have to first believe that God is God. Once you believe in God and confess that his son Jesus is Lord over your life you have put on the Helmet of Salvation. This helmet covers the area where our minds are located. We must keep our minds protected so that it only receives instructions from the government of Heaven in our hearts. This area is critical because it represents your head which is our central location of operation for our bodies. This area is where the battle for our souls takes place. Next, as we hide the Word in our hearts, we put on the Breastplate of Righteousness. The breastplate protects the Word of Wisdom which is the fiery core of our stability. This breastplate represents that through Jesus, the Word of Truth, we have been made righteous. Now that we know the truth we are not ashamed because this fiery truth adorns our loins. As we gain more knowledge of the Truth of God we gain more understanding of that truth. When we understand God this brings us tranquility which equips our feet with peace. This peace of God that surpasses all understanding allows us to stand where there is no visible footing. Jesus gives us this peace that surpasses all understanding which creates an atmosphere of inexpressible Joy. These spiritual atmospheric layers provide you with the defense to withstand and ward off every one of Satan's tricks or schemes.

Here the explanation given by God is from the inside out or upside down in the eyes of man. If you haven't noticed it by now, this book entitled His Marvelous Light was written from the inside out, or upside down because upside down is right side up to God. This is interesting because scientists have proven that our eyes see images upside down. God gives you an image upside down on purpose so that when your brain processes it, it will be right-side up. He does this because our perception has been perverted by sin, so we tend to turn things that are upside down, right side up, and things that are right side up, upside down. God gave His Word in a way that the carnal mind could see that God's way is the total opposite of Satan's way.

After the carnal man realizes the error in his ways he can now choose the right way through repentance. When you confess Christ, you allow God's mind to take over your mind and you begin to see things the right way instead of your way. Now that you know God's mind, you will notice that the mountain that you thought you were climbing to success was actually a deep valley that leads to death. The Word of God says there is a way that seems right to a man but ends in death.

We can't have an atmosphere of peace and joy if we don't have a good solid understanding of God's word in our hearts. We must first go down, in order to come up. The first shall be last and the last shall be first. The humble shall be exalted. We must be humble to understand God's ways from the Throne Room of Humility which is at the center of the rainbow. As stated earlier from the center of humility in the middle of the rainbow God looks out at the world. God's perspective of seeing from the inside out differs from man's perverted perspective of the world from the outside in. Man looks at the outward appearance but God searches the heart within.

When we intentionally cultivate our lives in humility, we make our own fleshly agenda small so that we won't block out the light of God's knowledge. This makes him Ruler over our lives by exalting Him by allowing His light within us to shine through us. Now instead of reflecting a false light like Satan, we can let the Holy Spirit's Fire within us to become the light that shines from the inside out. This is the same light that most people call a halo that surrounded Jesus that was visible from time to time. This was evidence of the Holy Spirit within him leading, protecting, comforting, guiding, and guarding him throughout his everyday life. These things resulted from Jesus not allowing His heart to be troubled, which kept him in a state of perfect peace.

God wants you to see that as long as you can keep your focus on him no matter what you are going through in this world, nothing can harm you. Your ability to stand comes from the solid rock of the revealed Word of God. This stance of peace in the face of adversity is the believer's impervious force field against Satan's forces. It's the protecting atmosphere that surrounds the rock that the gates of Hell cannot prevail against.

It wasn't just the fact that Peter hid the Word in His heart that made his rock untouchable, but it was the fact Peter understood the Word that made it powerful. Jesus knew that since Peter understood who He was, meant that Peter had been listening to the very still, small voice of God. This still small voice was spoken by none other than the Holy Spirit. God's Holy Spirit let Peter in on this sacred secret. We must be established on the firm foundation of understanding as believers to have a sound mind.

This is what this book is all about. Knowing God by having a firm understanding of Him and as a result of this comprehension, all those secret, mysterious ways of God are understood as well. Then the more you understand about your Father God in Heaven the more power you will have to be His manifested sons in the earth.

God is saying if you just read my Word and not know me then you are like the religious Pharisees having a form of Godliness. Or you can read My Word and listen to My Holy Spirit in order to understand my ways and be My sons. That rock that is given to each of us is a rock of understanding, representing the fact that God has made us his sons and has renamed us accordingly. God wants to talk to us and have us understand him just like he understands us.

Matthew 11:27 KJV
No one knows the Son, except the Father; neither does anyone know the Father, except the Son, and he to whom the Son desires to reveal him.

This is God's ultimate goal of reconciliation and Jesus' heart's desire to reveal His Father to us. The fact that Peter understood, excited Jesus and He immediately blessed him because he who was once the son of Barjonas was now a son of God. Jesus renamed him, Peter, meaning the rock. The Rock is a sealed covenant that God gives to us as Abraham's descendants. This rock is like a modern book or an ancient scroll. In this book is everything one needs to become a child of Abraham and a son of God. The book was written in reverse meaning the end of the book is what God did first. First God designed Abraham's destiny around

Himself and placed Abraham's destiny within a designated place. God orchestrated Abraham's destiny to be achieved through his son or his legacy. This place designated for Abraham's son Isaac was named Mount Moriah. The Mountain is Jesus the rock Himself representing the Son of God. This Rock is the impenetrable cover of the book. If you could picture the cover of the book it is open and Abraham's destiny that is designed around God is placed on the last page. Going down through a section of books that make up this one book from back to front you will find Jesus the seed of God. Continuing in this book from back to front through the second series of books you will find Abraham's seed, Isaac. As God closed this book He told his servant Abraham to sacrifice a ram and with the blood of that ram, He sealed the book. Abraham then dedicated this designated place called Mt Moriah by giving it back to God. Then Abraham renamed this place "Jehovah Provides" named after the contents that God placed within the book. The rock that is the covenant between God and Abraham was given to man as a written scroll. However, the healing hidden secrets of this book can't be decrypted by reading it but only through interpretation as the Holy Spirit reveals it. Now in order for mankind to receive this revelation, He must work out the process of this covenant in reverse in order to get to the Father. First, mankind must break the seal by accepting the blood of the lamb which is the Son of God. The only way to get to the Father is through the Son. Then He becomes an heir of Abraham through Jesus who was given for Isaac. Next, the seed of God is planted in man's heart which is this rock in the form of the Word of God. This also represents the two stone tablets of the Law given to Moses. Planting these stones of the law within the hearts of men is symbolic of God's grace that continues to perfect men as they fall short of keeping this perfect law. Grace was given because Jesus known as the Perfect Word of the Law dwelled with men as a man allowing a Perfect Law to feel the pains of imperfection. As a result, Jesus who is our Perfect High Priest can be touched with the feelings of our infirmities. Now when we accept Jesus and enter into this covenant the stony heart of the Law that was given to Abraham by God now has been dedicated back to God by Abraham. Now God multiplies that stone back to Abraham's descendants through Jesus as a heart of flesh making them sons of God. Then the Holy Spirit reveals the mind of God and grows this new heart of flesh as one disciplines his body to be submissive to the mind of the Holy Spirit. This inheritance of Abraham is the firm rock known as the sound mind of God manifested through us.

The rock of wisdom, knowledge, and understanding, as well as Power, Love, and a Sound mind is God planting his seed in you. It is in the form of a seed because you have to be planted in order to grow. Now that our Guide, Comforter, Counselor, and Protector has been planted within us we can now provide protection for others who haven't learned to stand on their faith. The word of God said the strong shall bear the infirmities of the weak, which means protection just like Jesus did for his disciples on that boat. Jesus' force field of peace not only changed the weather to the calm of the Kingdom of Heaven but also caused the Kingdom to defy time and space and instantly they were on the other side. Let us humble ourselves in order that the name of the Lord can be exalted. His name is a strong tower that the righteous run into and are saved. If we go down and humble ourselves in order that Jesus may be lifted, He will draw all men unto Him.

As we mentioned before, like the Tower of Babel, man having one language erected a tower as a testament to himself. The Name of The Lord is the Tower which is built by having the common language of praise. This is exemplified when each man and woman in the body of Christ has joined together by exalting the next person's gift over theirs. This is the principle of humility where one humbles himself in order to edify the next person. Then in turn the next person humbles himself to edify the one that humbled himself for him. As a result, everyone is edified because in our humility where we are weak our brother makes us strong. Hence we have all sufficiency in all things. This is Completion through Endurance, not Elimination through Competition. This is how the Tower of The Lord will be built.

This tower is constructed by the stones representing those that have accepted the Lord Jesus Christ as their personal Lord and Savior coming together collectively by submitting to the government of Heaven. We are humbled by cultivating ourselves in every aspect of our daily lives, bringing every thought, will, and emotion under subjection to God in the secret place of the Holy of Holies within our hearts. This is what the word of God is calling you to acknowledge him as the governing ruler of your individual lives so He can direct your path.

First, we need to erase all opinions about God and other people. Then we need to stop being easily offended by casting down all our imaginations and every high and lofty thing of our flesh. Instead, we give all our cares to God so that he can not only fix them but perfect them.

When we reach this level of humility, we realize that it's our flesh that wants to lead all things and rule over all situations in the house of God. We also realize that those forced to become unnoticed and take the same humble position as Jesus will become the keystone. The keystone is the stone that the builders rejected like Joseph who represents the black people and Jesus that was cast down. However, while they were down the gift gave them the opportunity to be elevated to a position of power.

When everyone searches for the minute errors of their own hearts and minds, they are making sure that their own house is in order with God. The truth is being revealed to us by the Holy Spirit in a Life-changing manner that makes our own individual souls free. This is a place where we can walk and talk with God individually. As His sons, we commune daily with God as Adam did in the Garden of Eden. This place is our own personal Kingdom of Heaven in our hearts. Then, and only then, will the people of the world see His irresistible light then taste of His fruit of Wisdom and know that it is good.

Now after we have made sure that we intentionally want to know God for ourselves, then we can truly come together as one heart, under one ruler, on one accord, bearing one language, and living in one culture, forming one huge Kingdom. When all these different stones get together under the same atmosphere, we can fuse together to form one big gigantic force field around us protecting us from all harm. Their intentions are now all aligned with the will of God by having the mind of the Holy Spirit that dwells in them all. This is why one can put a thousand to flight and two ten thousand. This Tower of Light that is formed is the place where the sons of God will run into to be saved from the terrors that must come to pass in the last days.

These Stones Shall Cry Out

We are familiar with the scripture where the Pharisees told Jesus to command his disciples to be quiet. Jesus replied to them as it is recorded in Luke19:39-44 NIV

39Some of the Pharisees in the crowd said to Jesus, "Teacher, rebuke your disciples!"

40"I tell you," he replied, "if they keep quiet, the stones will cry out."

41As he approached Jerusalem and saw the city, he wept over it 42and said, "If you, even you, had only known on this day what would bring you peace—but now it is hidden from your eyes. 43The days will come upon you when your enemies will build an embankment against you and encircle you and hem you in on every side. 44They will dash you to the ground, you and the children within your walls. They will not leave one stone on another, because you did not recognize the time of God's coming to you."

Jesus wasn't talking about natural stones. Later on in verse 42, he gives us a hint of what he is actually referring to after he had wept for the City and told them if you, even you had only known on this day what would bring you peace, but now it is hidden from your eyes. God has hidden some things from humanity on purpose as part of his covert plan to build his temple back on the stone that the builders rejected. As you know by now, this stone is the spiritual stone represented by the physical, onyx stone of Joseph. This is the only stone that was hidden by God that would eventually hold together all the other stones in His spiritual family of Peace. These spiritual stones that Jesus was speaking of were the twelve stones of the ephod. They represent the spiritual gifting that he gave to each tribe of Israel to give him praise. We praise God through our spiritual gifts. Jesus said, "if I don't allow my disciples to praise me, that very thing that represents the very essence of their spiritual gifting would start to praise me."

This is how God plans to construct his spiritual Tower of Praise that is totally opposite of the tower of pride that Satan tried to build at Babel. We also know that which was hidden was the true Identity of Black People. Why did the temple fall in the first place?

The Temple fell because it was not founded upon the rock of a people who had been rejected by their brothers and hidden by God. These brothers that rejected this stone were the builders of the current temple that represent the Church of God, and Jerusalem which represents the governments of the world. Broken-hearted, Jesus cried while saying the very one you rejected is the one that will bring you peace. Jesus was not just speaking of himself; but He was also saying that as long as you reject the stone of your brother that I chose for you to build on, you will crumble and fall. The keystone is the only stone with the right shape and density which is humility that is able to hold all of the other stones together. Jesus was weeping for these people because he knew the pain of their rejection like Joseph when he wept from the pit.

In verses, forty- three through forty-four of this passage Jesus speaks prophetically about how the enemy will build up forts and raid Jerusalem if they don't recognize who God has sent to them. Cain killed Abel because he considered him a threat in the realm of the Father. The religious sect considered Jesus a threat, so they had him crucified in the realm of the Son. We enter the realm of the Holy Spirit represented by Jesus entering the city of Jerusalem. Then we enter the Temple like the spirit of Adam being breathed by the Holy Spirit into his newly created body. Jerusalem and the Holy Temple represent those who will not be able to recognize their brother as their peacemaker and sustainer through troublesome times. Just like Joseph noticed that his brothers didn't recognize him as he talked to them after he became the Prince of Egypt.

The Temple represented the modern-day Church of Christ and Jesus represents the Black People. The Church will not recognize the one that God put into Power for their sake in the last days. The world will become in many ways like it was in the time of Joseph. However, the Black man will be placed into power and become imperative to the survival of the Nations.

He will also be providing the necessary provisions for the Church of Christ in perilous days. They will become second in power over what will be considered a heathen nation. The Black People will hold true to their Christian values as Joseph did at Potiphar's House, in Prison, and the Palace. They will not compromise their values for anyone.

The modern Church's rejection of Jesus is due to her not being able to recognize the move of the Holy Spirit that places black people in a position of power and wealth for the sake of all mankind. For this reason, Jesus will dismantle His physical Church as we know it as He stated in Matthew 24:1-2(TLB). The other buildings that stood off from the main Temple represented the many different views points that have separated the Church into many religious sects. These differences in opinions are the reason why Jesus was unrecognizable as He approached the religious groups of His day. They already had their own view of how Jesus should look and the manner in which He should carry Himself. How Joseph was presented to his brothers as the Prince of Egypt greatly differed from the mental picture that they had of him as a slave. As for the Black People that Joseph represents the way they will be presented to the Church and the governments of the world will differ greatly from how they were perceived originally.

Matthew 24:1-2 TLB
24 As Jesus was leaving the Temple grounds, his disciples came along and wanted to take him on a tour of the various Temple buildings.
2 But he told them, "All these buildings will be knocked down, with not one stone left on top of another!"

The dismantling of the old church is a process that started as soon as Jesus walked through the door of the Temple.

Matthew 21:12-13 TLB
12 Jesus went into the Temple, drove out the merchants, and knocked over the money changers' tables and the stalls of those selling doves.
13 "The Scriptures say my Temple is a place of prayer," he declared, "but you have turned it into a den of thieves."

First, he said that my house shall be called a house of prayer and you have turned it into a den of thieves. After that, he started the process of dismantling the form of Godliness that was on the tables as a form of bribery from politicians wanting the church to cover their evil deeds with the name of God. The church had become a den of thieves. Through its form of Godliness, the church promised peace to these workers of iniquity represented by the selling of doves. These stones were represented by the coins hitting the floor as Jesus turned over the tables of the money changers. Not one stone or coin was left on the top of the other. The tables that held up the coins represented the platform on which the church stood. Jesus was demonstrating through manifestation that the Church would no longer depend on political parties or the platforms of politicians for gain.

The word of God would be the four pillars to the platform that held up the CHURCH and the government would be on Him who rules righteously from that platform. We call this platform the Pulpit and the person who will rule is Jesus, the Son of the Living God.

Yes, black people will be called to carry this weight of Government for a while. Just like he carried Jesus' cross until it was time for Jesus to return to take over to rule justly and righteously.

The Church will be rebuilt again in three days using the proper keystone. It will not be built by physical hands but upon the revealed Word of God. As a result, the Church will be not able to base the likeness of Jesus on a carnal preconceived notion of Him, but on the full knowledge of Jesus as He is revealed to His Church by the Holy Spirit. The Church will grow like the stone that grew into a mountain in Isaiah. His Church will tower above the earth with each person, from each nationality, adding their stone to the Tower of the Lord as they did to the Tower of Babel. This Tower will be a testament to God as He resides in the middle of this true manifestation of praise. The stones of each person's spiritual gift given to them by the Holy Ghost are all in submission to the Father. The Living Stone that God gave you is in the perfect image of God the Father. This is your heart and soul just like He is our heart and soul. We all hold up the name of the Lord a fortress that the righteous run into and are safe from all harm. This will not be a literal building because everyone is spread out physically. Collectively our spirits are being connected in perfect order like it was promised by God in the rainbow. We are all a part of that seven-fold Spirit working as one organism that makes up the Body or the Bride of Christ. All of our hearts collectively as living stones will form the Living Stone called the Mountain of God, and out of that Living Stone will flow the issues of hearts.

John 7:37-39 NIV
37On the last and greatest day of the festival, Jesus stood and said in a loud voice, "Let anyone who is thirsty come to me and drink. 38Whoever believes in me, as Scripture has said, rivers of living water will flow from within them." 39By this he meant the Spirit, whom those who believed in him were later to receive. Up to that time the Spirit had not been given, since Jesus had not yet been glorified.

These rivers of living waters that flow from our hearts will form the River of Life that allows God's will to be done on earth. This river is the Holy Spirit that will flow from our willing hearts through the disciplined and obedient river bed of our carnal man into the natural. This carnal river bed is the way of the Lord that John the Baptist told us to prepare for Him. Through us, the Holy Spirit will literally heal the sick, raise the dead, and free all that are oppressed. The un-denied power of the Holy Spirit will enable us as the manifested sons of God to do greater works than our Lord Jesus Christ. Amen

John 14:12 King James Version
12 Verily, verily, I say unto you, He that believeth on me, the works that I do shall he do also; AND GREATER WORKS THAN THESE SHALL HE DO; because I go unto my Father.

ABOUT THE AUTHOR

Willard D.Broughton is a minister, prophet, teacher, and motivational speaker with a platform not based on religion but on understanding the scriptures by the light of revelation knowledge imparted by the Holy Spirit. His scripturally founded teachings paint mental pictures that compel people to acknowledge the mind of God when reading the Holy Scriptures rather than forming an opinion about His unthinkable preeminence. He is also the co-founder of (L.I.T.) Living In Truth Ministries an evangelistic organization that focuses on how to authentically become sons of God not just by Spiritual relation but by knowing the mind of God to manifest our Royal power-filled family traits on earth. In his new book, God gave Willard the Secrets to eradicating the confines of governmental oppression and social injustice by using His Marvelous Light to expose how it conflicts with the mind of the believer. These secrets have also illuminated the mystery of why God shaded mankind in different colors and the hidden history of black people in the Bible. Being a gifted electrician and electronics technician Willard and his wife successfully ran a satellite services business for over five years. Currently employed by a major carrier He likes to unwind through reading, creative carpentry, and the sizzle of a juicy steak on an open grill. While residing in the beautiful State of Alabama he enjoys life with His wife and family as God graces Willard with prophetic revelation knowledge to write potential world-changing BEST SELLERS.